PRAISE FOR *THAT THEY LIVED*

"*That They Lived* is an instant classic. Words and images, the past and the future, weave back and forth in a stunningly original children's book, until we see and hear the American Dream becoming an American reality as the young people depicted—and the young people reading—come to know their history and their power. People of all ages will enjoy this brilliant, necessary, charming, and inspiring volume. Parents and teachers will find inspirations for endless activities inspired by these pages."

—ALICE RANDALL, professor of African-American children's literature at Vanderbilt University and author of *The Diary of B. B. Bright, Possible Princess* (winner of the Phillis Wheatley Book Award) and *Black Bottom Saints*

"It is true that children can only become what they see. *That They Lived* provides that window on the world of African Americans who achieved greatness, often against the odds. Riley's words combined with Smith-Jones's beautiful and touching photography make these history-makers accessible for children and adults alike."

—TERRI LEE FREEMAN, President, National Civil Rights Museum

"*That They Lived* transforms Frederick Douglass from a historical figure into a courageous soul who helped turn the nation against slavery. Aretha Franklin is no longer just a voice but a young woman who overcame tragedy and prejudice on her way to success. *That They Lived* makes the stories of these courageous African Americans come alive, making it possible for young people of all colors to see how they, too, can change the world."

—JERRY MITCHELL, author of *Race Against Time*

"There is no other book about African American lives like *That They Lived*. Riley and Smith-Jones have revisited twenty-one historic figures to demonstrate that whatever fame or greatness one achieves, everyone was a child once. How wonderful to learn of the childhoods of icons from Douglass to Obama, Wells to Hamer, and so many more. The book gleams with the sheer variety of Black life and ambition. The photographs are magic. This is for young readers, but really for all of us since we all came from somewhere."

—DAVID W. BLIGHT, Yale University, author of Pulitzer Prize–winning *Frederick Douglass: Prophet of Freedom*

"The moment my son begins to read, I will give him this fascinating book. The chance to experience our Black heroes' younger lives gives our children the confidence to pursue the greatness of their own. We know how the world sees us, so it's essential to ensure that our children see themselves as powerful before sending them out in it. Rochelle and Cristi's book is an elegant and profound means to help them do just that."

—QASIM BASIR, filmmaker

"Mixing words with images, *That They Lived* introduces African American luminaries anew through the eyes of a girl named Lola and a boy named Caleb. Their game of dress-up is not merely play, explains Lola's mother, photographer Cristi Smith-Jones. Their imaginings are paired here with Rochelle Riley's vivid biographies, inviting us all to see ourselves in the Black Americans who have transformed our world. This book invites young people to dream big and then fashion themselves into the next generation of change agents."

—MARTHA S. JONES, author of *Vanguard: How Black Women Broke Barriers, Won the Vote, and Insisted on Equality for All*

THAT THEY LIVED

THAT THEY LIVED

AFRICAN AMERICANS WHO CHANGED THE WORLD

Rochelle Riley and Cristi Smith-Jones

A Painted Turtle Book

Detroit

ISBN 978-0-8143-4754-6 (paperback); ISBN 978-0-8143-4755-3 (ebook)

LIBRARY OF CONGRESS CONTROL NUMBER: 2020944274

Published with support from the Arthur L. Johnson Fund
for African American Studies.

That They Lived was made possible through a grant provided by the
Community Foundation for Southeast Michigan.

Community Foundation

FOR SOUTHEAST MICHIGAN

Wayne State University Press
Leonard N. Simons Building
4809 Woodward Avenue
Detroit, Michigan 48201-1309

Visit us online at wsupress.wayne.edu

To every child who aspires to be great . . . when they grow up

Contents

Foreword

In June 2019, I ran into the renowned writer Rochelle Riley at a local car wash. I first met her in 2015 when I was in the fourth grade and was a finalist in a writing competition she hosted. It was definitely a blast from the past when I saw her again.

I was on the phone with a customer, so she told my mom about the latest book she was completing on important African Americans who had changed the world. And my mom told her how I had started my own business making natural body butters and body scrubs.

After I finished my conversation, Ms. Riley congratulated me on all my hard work. Then, all of a sudden, she asked me if I would write the foreword for her book!

I remember growing up and my mother and father—and, most importantly, my grandmother—making sure that I knew my roots. I remember reading different books on African-American culture. I was at the Charles H. Wright Museum of African American History so much that we should have gotten memberships. I even got the chance to experience the fiftieth anniversary of the March on Selma by traveling to Selma, Alabama. I had the opportunity to walk across the Edmund Pettus Bridge, where many civil rights activists put their lives on the line for our right to vote. I felt proud and powerful as I placed one foot in front of the other, knowing that my ancestors once walked before me. We also visited the 16th Street Baptist Church in Birmingham, Alabama, where four little Black girls were killed in a hate bombing in 1963. I felt a sense of discomfort knowing that four innocent girls near my age were killed because of the color of their skin. So, I am aware of the past struggles and triumphs of African-American people.

I was so excited about Ms. Riley's new book, and I was thrilled that she asked me to write the foreword. I had only one question in my mind: "Why me?"

Well, I had a second question. What Ms. Riley didn't know was that I didn't have a clue what a foreword was. But I wasn't going to let her down. I looked up the definition: "a short introduction to a book, typically by a person other than the author."

Then I read the book. And I instantly fell in love with it!

Photographer Cristi Smith-Jones's story about how this journey began was absolutely remarkable. It sounded like a fairy tale. What a great idea it was to take pictures of her young daughter honoring different African-American women in history. It led to major outreach around the world. I felt a connection with Ms. Smith-Jones's daughter because when I returned from Selma, I was so amazed by what I had witnessed that I created a pictorial quilt with the faces of African-American women in the civil rights movement.

This is not just a book about different African Americans. It has information that museums don't even have. Not only did the facts in the stories capture my attention, but the pictures featuring Ms. Smith-Jones's daughter and Ms. Riley's grandson were oh-so-cute. But they were also powerful.

Frederick Douglass was one of my favorites. The lesson that he taught us is this: Do not give up on your goals. Then your goals can become your dream, and your dream will become your reality.

I related to these leaders' stories in so many ways. When I first started my business, things were not always great for me. As a young entrepreneur, I got used to people wondering: "What has this little kid got going on?" Well, that little kid had a mission.

In 2015, my mother was diagnosed with breast cancer. Our family became more aware of the chemicals we put on and in our bodies. I started making all-natural deodorant with my grandmother and decided that I also wanted to make lotions and scrubs. I researched the various natural ingredients that I could use to moisturize skin, smell amazing, and be long-lasting.

Today my mom is a survivor! I'm so glad she gets to watch me work.

And it is a real job. I always ask my customers to give me positive and negative comments. I want the advice. I want the opinions. The feedback is not great all the time. But I know that I can't cry and that I can't just drop everything and quit. I know I have to keep reaching for my goal and strive for greatness. I remember what President Barack Obama taught us, which Ms. Riley also included in the book: Anything is possible when you believe, when you have hope, and when you want to change the world.

I'm sure everyone's mother, father, or family has taught them that they can do anything they put their mind to. That is the message that will stick with me my whole life. That is what makes me believe that if I put my mind to it, I can do anything and I can make a mark on this world— just like all of the people in this book did. Ms. Riley tells their stories from when they were children. That makes me believe it's possible.

I would like to thank Rochelle Riley and Cristi Smith-Jones for positively influencing me and expanding my knowledge of these remarkable individuals in history who have had a long-lasting influence on American history. One day I hope to change the world and make my ancestors proud by motivating young women like me to reach for their dreams. I want girls to be aware that we come from generations of successful people and that success is in our DNA. Then maybe one day, someone will read this about me:

When Aniya Floyd was 11 years old, she was a sixth-grade student at Detroit's University Prep Science & Math School. But when she was 14, she started her own skin care company. And when she's 30, she hopes to sell her products worldwide and be an inspiration to children everywhere who want to reach their goals.

ANIYA FLOYD, 14

CEO, A's Scrub & Rub Natural Body Butters and Scrubs

Freshman, Cass Technical High School, Detroit

Note from the Authors

America has become enthralled with "hidden figures" in its history: African Americans whose contributions were ignored because of racism and discrimination. This book honors the prominent African Americans who are known, whose stories are shared during Black History Month, but who, despite their accomplishments, still are not treated with the respect and adulation they deserve as a part of a continuing American history. Their stories should be told every month, all year.

This collection of biographical, inspirational essays is for young readers, their families, and teachers. We created this book to honor the heroes we know and tell the story of their journeys from childhood.

It is offered at a time and age when our young people are deciding who they can be, regardless of their color.

We want to show them that every important or powerful or talented or beautiful person in the world was once a child.

Cristi's Story

One afternoon in January, my daughter Lola, who was five at the time, came home from school and told my husband and me about Dr. Martin Luther King Jr.

She had watched a video about him in honor of the upcoming Martin Luther King Jr. Day.

I was surprised at how well she seemed to grasp concepts such as segregation and the "dream" that Dr. King had.

It got me thinking, and with Black History Month right around the corner, I decided that it was an opportune time to begin teaching her about some of the women who paved the way for so many.

Using Lola's love of playing dress-up as a teaching tool, I decided that for every day of Black History Month, I would dress her as an important figure in our history and photograph her. Armed mostly with articles of clothing and props that we owned, we began.

I was blown away by how well Lola was able to emote, capturing the spirit of each woman. I shared the photos on social media, in the hope that our family and friends would enjoy the journey with us. I had informed Lola's kindergarten teacher, Teresa Sawyer, about the project and was delighted to learn that she was sharing the photos, as well as information about the women Lola was portraying, with the rest of the class every day.

What began as a teaching opportunity for my daughter was now helping other children learn, and they loved seeing her transform each day.

I posted the images on social media, and the initial response was supportive and positive. To my surprise, my friends and family began to share the photos across social media as well.

Toward the end of the month, our little passion project caught the attention of several news outlets in the Seattle area. We were featured on our local news, and from there the project seemed to spread like wildfire.

We were honored to find out that we had made the front page of the *Seattle Times*. At that point, our photos began to go viral on social media. They were trending on Twitter and we found ourselves doing interviews with major media outlets, such as CNN, NBC, and *People* magazine.

Videos about our project were garnering millions of views. After reaching a national level, the photos of Lola began to be shared internationally as well, reaching as far as Japan, Britain, and Australia. I received messages from people daily who were inspired by Lola.

With all of the attention that our project received came commendations from influential people, like Senator Kamala Harris and Cornell Williams Brooks, then-president of the National Association for the

Advancement of Colored People (NAACP). We were also praised by people we honored, like Dr. Mae Jemison, the first Black woman to travel into space.

A'Lelia Bundles enjoyed our tribute to her great-great-grandmother Madam C. J. Walker and sent Lola a care package with books and memorabilia about her.

After seeing our tribute to ballerina Misty Copeland, some lovely people from the University of Washington invited us to see Misty speak and to meet her. Lola had the honor of joining a few other little girls onstage to present Misty with flowers.

After Black History Month ended, we were contacted by the International Center of Photography in New York. Officials there enjoyed the photo series so much that they projected the images onto the windows of their museum. We traveled to New York to see it. It was such a beautiful experience to see my little Lola portraying such indomitable women, on display for all to see.

As the whirlwind began to settle down, I was left feeling immensely grateful and humbled by the entire experience.

I am a stay-at-home wife and mother turned amateur photographer, and I could never have imagined that we would reach so many people. It felt as though we were continuing the legacies of women who made it possible for generations of children to achieve their dreams. They have already affected Lola's life, and I hope that Lola carries those legacies with her as she forges her own path.

Rochelle's Story

I am a journalist. I have been a journalist since I was eight years old. I spent more than 30 years professionally chronicling the lives and actions of people famous and infamous. I have worked at newspapers across the country, writing about education, politics, culture, and children. I was a newspaper columnist for most of that time. I offered opinions on everything from global affairs to school lunches.

I also am a social mediologist. I spend hours each week on Facebook, Twitter, and Instagram, not only because it is necessary to keep up with news and popular culture but also because the World Wide Web is an amazing playground. It makes it easier to study social trends and keep my finger on the pulse of American readers.

So in February 2017, when photos began showing up on Facebook of a tiny face carrying the beauty and grace of famous African-American women, I was immediately smitten. I was in awe of this little girl who could so powerfully honor the history and struggle and achievement of much older women, of women that every child should know.

I contacted the young wife and mother who posted the photos of her daughter, Lola, and asked whether I could come out to visit.

I traveled to Kent, Washington, outside Seattle, and spent a day hanging out with Cristi's family. I talked to her about melding those photos with words that could inspire children. I wanted us to teach future leaders about the accomplishments and contributions of African Americans to America. Together, we would encourage them to reach for similar heights and to remind them that every important, every famous, every celebrated person, was once a child.

I talked to Cristi about my one-woman campaign to make America's public schools teach a complete history of America rather than the segregated histories we teach now. My campaign, *ONE AMERICA, ONE HISTORY*, begins with the single idea that our goal should not be to uncover hidden figures. Our goal should be to stop hiding them.

I returned to Kent months later with my grandson, Caleb, so Cristi could honor African-American men through his face. We chose men whose impacts were historic and whose words, ideas, and ideals were lasting.

His favorite photo shoot was of Frederick Douglass because, well, he loved the hair.

Cristi and I want to help all children of all colors and backgrounds see African Americans as they are: as varied as their names, as smart as their achievements, and as strong as their history.

This book—and subsequent books featuring young children from across the nation as scientists, business leaders, sports stars, film stars, educators, civil rights leaders, inventors, explorers, political leaders, religious leaders, military heroes, and artists—will prove that African Americans have, for centuries, lived and achieved in music, film, sports, politics, religion, the arts, science, and other fields. These books, designed for children, will fill in gaps in the history that they—and we all—have been taught for generations.

For African-American children, it will prove that they are more than descendants of the enslaved. For children of all backgrounds, it will make clear that Black children are more than descendants of the enslaved.

We want to shine a light on the best of us, as well as the rest of us—inventors, abolitionists, leaders, and heroes—to show that they lived and that they achieved and helped make America—and the world—great.

And they—we—still do.

MUHAMMAD ALI

Muhammad Ali would grow up to be one of the greatest athletes in history, a man admired for his fight for political freedom as much as for his boxing.

But before he was known as "The Greatest," he was a 12-year-old boy named Cassius Marcellus Clay Jr., growing up in Louisville, Kentucky. And he was the victim of a crime.

Someone stole his bicycle.

It was October 1954.

Cassius, the son of Odessa and Cassius Clay Sr., rode his new red bike downtown to attend a showcase for Black businesses. Louisville did not allow Black-owned businesses to participate in the city's main showcase. So the Black showcase was a real draw for Black children and families.

Cassius and his friend left their bikes outside to go sample food. When it was time to go home, he went outside and realized that his new red, $60 Schwinn was gone. A stranger told him to go back into the building and find a white police officer named Joe Martin.

Officer Martin ran a boxing gym that Cassius had never seen before. He told the officer what happened and said: "When I find whoever took my bike, I'm gonna whup him."

Martin, who had been an amateur boxer, looked at Cassius and told him if he was going to beat somebody, he'd better learn how to fight first. He told Cassius that he could come to the gym every day after school. The next weekend, when Cassius saw Officer Martin's gym on television, he decided to be a boxer.

No one will ever know what might have happened to young Cassius if someone hadn't stolen his bike and if he hadn't met Joe Martin. But it happened, and he did. And the two began a journey that would change a young boy's life.

From that week, Cassius became focused on one goal: being the best boxer in the world.

Before school, he ran around the park near his house wearing steel-toed boots. After school, he went to his part-time job sweeping floors, dusting shelves, and mowing the lawn at the Nazareth College Library. At 6 p.m., he headed to Officer Martin's gym to train. At 8 p.m., he went to a second gym just for Black boxers and trained until midnight. The next day, he started all over again.

Every day, Cassius raced the school bus to school. He jumped rope between classes. He shadow-boxed in the boys' bathroom mirror. At the gym, he practiced jabs and hooks. He did push-ups. He did knee bends. And he practiced ducking and moving.

Cassius stopped eating hamburgers, French fries, and other junk food. He drank milk with a raw egg, and he adopted a motto: *Be dedicated, concentrate, pay the price.*

His principal at Central High School introduced him to other students as the next heavyweight champion of the world.

By 1958, he was on his way. That year, he won the Golden Gloves Light Heavyweight championship. Two years later, he won a gold medal at the Summer Olympics in Rome.

A few months after that, he turned pro and won his first fight in front of 6,000 fans in Louisville.

Cassius then focused on the dream he had claimed years before. He wanted to be the youngest man to win a heavyweight boxing championship.

In 1962, when he was 18, he began building his career as a boxer—and a talker. He earned the nickname the Louisville Lip because of his bragging. Boxers didn't like it, but fans loved it. Some reporters called him Mighty Mouth.

But he backed it up.

In 1961, he fought eight times and won every fight. He knocked out opponents in six of those fights. By 1964, Cassius earned the chance to fight the heavyweight champion, a man named Sonny Liston. Cassius created a phrase that was heard across the country and is still said today: "Float like a butterfly, sting like a bee."

More than 400 reporters from 17 countries covered the fight. It was a hard battle. Cassius wanted to quit but his trainer, a man named Angelo Dundee, told him "No."

Fights usually last 15 rounds. After the sixth round, Sonny Liston said his shoulder hurt. He refused to continue the fight.

Cassius became heavyweight champion.

Cassius fought and won many more boxing matches. But his greatest fight wasn't in the boxing ring.

Shortly after he beat Sonny Liston, Cassius announced that he was becoming a Muslim and a member of the Nation of Islam. He said he would not answer to the name Cassius Clay because it was a slave name. He began using the name that Nation of Islam leader Elijah Muhammad gave him: Muhammad Ali. A year later, he defeated Sonny Liston again.

But America was watching a bigger fight, a war between two countries: South Vietnam and North Vietnam. Russia, which was America's enemy, supported North Vietnam. So, America began sending soldiers to help South Vietnam fight. Young men across the country were forced to join the military. The military wanted Muhammad, too.

But Muhammad refused to go. He said, "I ain't got nothing against them Vietcong."

Officials who granted boxing licenses took away Muhammad's license. He could not fight anywhere in America.

His career was over.

For a time.

So, Muhammad did other things.

He spoke on college campuses about his Muslim beliefs, against the war in Vietnam, and against racial discrimination.

He got married.

But he still could not box.

He was convicted in 1967 of dodging the draft into the Army. His attorneys fought the case. Meanwhile, Muhammad was kicked out of the Nation of Islam for refusing to give up boxing for Islam. His Islamic leaders felt that sports were a sin that led to violence and bad choices.

But all Muhammad wanted to do was box.

In September 1970, the city of Atlanta gave him a license to fight. He fought at Morehouse College in front of 3,000 fans. One month later, a New York court ruled that banning Muhammad from boxing violated his rights.

He went back in the ring and won fight after fight. But everyone was waiting for the big fight. It would be called the "Fight of the Century." His opponent was Joe Frazier, considered by some to be the greatest of all time.

Joe was undefeated, and so was Muhammad.

Joe won the fight in 15 rounds. He took the heavyweight title from Muhammad.

Seven weeks later, on June 28, 1971, the U.S. Supreme Court ruled in Muhammad's favor and said he did not have to be drafted into the military. The vote was 8 to 0. Muhammad won that fight out of the ring. He won many more fights in the ring, including the 1974 "Rumble in the Jungle," where he won the heavyweight title by beating George Foreman. He also fought two more legendary bouts with Frazier. One was the famous "Thrilla in Manila" in the Philippines in 1975.

In February 1978, he fought Leon Spinks. Leon was 24, Muhammad was 36. Leon won, and took the title from Muhammad. But months later, they fought again, and Muhammad won. He became the only boxer in history to win the heavyweight title three times.

In his life, Muhammad kept fighting when people said he should stop. After his last loss in December 1981 against an unknown fighter named Trevor Berbick, he finally listened and said, "I'll never fight again."

For years, Muhammad led life away from the spotlight, attending autograph sessions and existing quietly on his farm in Berrien Springs, Michigan. But in July 1996, during the Summer Olympics in Los Angeles, an American swimmer named Janet Evans carried the Olympic torch into the stadium and up a ramp toward the cauldron where it would light the flame to open the games.

But she didn't light the cauldron. She reached her torch toward the hands of the most famous man, the most famous athlete, in the world.

He was 54 and visibly shaking, showing signs of Parkinson's disease, an illness marked by tremors and stiff arms and legs.

But Muhammad Ali touched the torch to the cauldron.

The fire erupted.

And the world cried.

When I met him in 1996, his steps and movements were slowed by Parkinson's. But his mind was sharp, his legacy was made. He showed the world—and all children—that only you decide what and who you want to be.

SHIRLEY CHISHOLM

Shirley Chisholm would grow up to be the first African-American woman elected to Congress and the first woman to campaign to be a major party nominee for president.

But when Shirley Anita Hill was three years old, her family was so poor that her parents sent their three daughters to live in another country.

Shirley was born November 30, 1924, in Brooklyn, New York. Her parents were Caribbean immigrants. Her mother was a seamstress and domestic worker, and her father worked in a factory. Because of their struggles to make ends meet, they sent Shirley and her two sisters to live with their grandmother in Barbados.

Shirley lived on the island until she was 10. She was an excellent student. She later praised the "strict, traditional British-style schools" on the island for her academic excellence.

She returned to Brooklyn and graduated from high school. She attended Brooklyn College and ran a day care while she earned a master's degree in early childhood education from Columbia University.

She also began working in politics. She convinced the parents of the children at a local day care to help elect a judge.

A decade later, she decided to run for office herself. She was elected to the New York State Assembly in 1964.

She soon became known for her fiery spirit and her efforts to help the poor.

In 1968, she ran for Congress. She said her opponent had not done enough for the poor. She also said he did not fight hard enough to keep women from being mistreated. She won by a 2 to 1 margin. But she talked about how hard that campaign was.

"I've always met more discrimination being a woman than being Black," she said. "Men are men."

Shirley spoke out across the country about how poorly women were treated. She once said, "Tremendous amounts of talent are being lost to our society just because that talent wears a skirt."

In 1972, she decided to campaign to be president of the United States. People made fun of her.

But Shirley was serious. She knew she was paving the way for others.

"The next time a woman runs, or a Black, or a Jew, or anyone from a group that the country is 'not ready' to elect to its highest office, I believe he or she will be taken seriously from the start," she said. "The door is not open yet, but it is ajar."

She also criticized her fellow congressional representatives who did not support her.

"I have grown to detest many of the white Northern liberals who are always ready with rhetoric about equal opportunity in jobs and education," she wrote in her book *The Good Fight*. "When the time comes to put the heat on, in committee and on the floor, and do something, like passing an amendment or increasing an appropriation, too many of these white knights turn up missing."

Shirley continued to work hard. And she was always true to herself and her motto, "unbought and unbossed."

When it was time for her to retire, she continued to train future leaders. She taught women's studies, sociology, and politics at Mount Holyoke College in South Hadley, Massachusetts.

Nancy Pelosi, a member of the U.S. House of Representatives, once said of Shirley that she would "long be remembered as a catalyst for change in America."

Shirley's words have remained true for anyone who wants to be in public office.

"Service is the rent that you pay for room on this earth," she said.

Shirley also knew the mark she made in American history.

"That I am a national figure because I was the first person in 192 years to be at once a congressman, Black, and a woman proves, I think, that our society is not yet either just or free," she said.

When Shirley retired for good, she moved to Florida. She had never owned a car, so she turned her two-car garage into a library with thousands of books. When reporters asked her how she wanted to be remembered, she said, "I'd like them to say that Shirley Chisholm had guts."

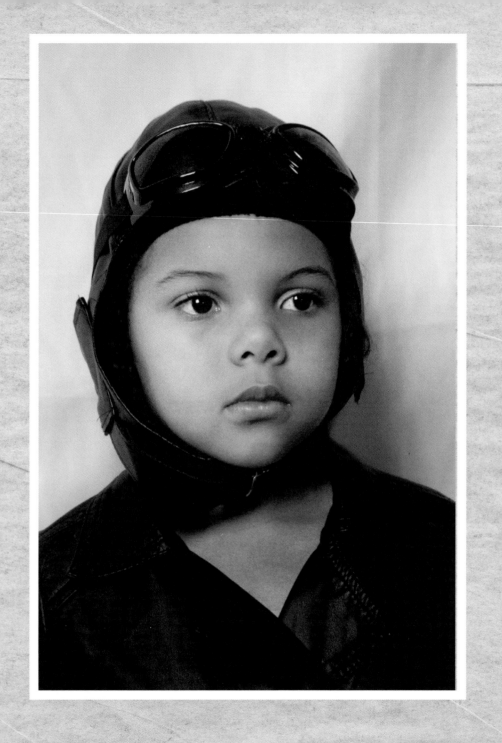

BESSIE COLEMAN

Bessie Coleman would grow up to become the first and most famous African-American aviator in history. Known as Brave Bessie, she would perform in stunt shows across the country and urge African Americans to fly.

But when she was 11, Bessie worked in the cotton fields with her family and was being raised by a single mother.

When she realized that she had a knack for math, Bessie knew her future wasn't in the fields. So her mother, Susan Coleman, encouraged her to work doing laundry to earn tuition money for college.

On Mondays, Bessie walked all over town collecting dirty laundry to bring home to clean. On Saturdays, she walked back around town to return the clean clothes. She earned between $4 and $8 every month and saved enough to enter the Colored Agricultural and Normal University in Langston, Oklahoma. But Bessie had to leave after a single term when she ran out of money. So she went back to doing laundry.

But she didn't do it for long.

Her brothers, Walter and John, had moved to Chicago. So when she turned 23, Bessie went to live with them and their wives in a neighborhood called the Black Belt. Walter was a Pullman porter at a time when racist treatment was commonplace. For instance, the Black porters could not sleep on the white sheets provided to white passengers. They had to use old sheets that had been dyed blue so white passengers would not accidentally use them.

Bessie learned how to manicure nails at the E. Burnham School of Beauty Culture. She worked at a shop on Black Wall Street. She soon got married. Eventually, all of the Colemans moved to Chicago.

America was fighting in World War I. When it ended in November 1918, people were talking about how French women were becoming pilots. Bessie noticed and said she was interested in flying. Her brother joked in the barbershop that there was no way African-American women could fly planes like French women.

Bessie set out to prove him wrong. But no U.S. flight schools would train her. Bessie later said, "I refused to take no for an answer." She had earned the respect of Black businessmen. Two of them were Robert Abbott, the publisher of the Black newspaper called the *Chicago*

Defender, and Jesse Binga, a Black banker. She moved to France and took flying lessons. After only seven months, she earned her license from the Fédération Aéronautique Internationale. She was the first Black woman to earn an international pilot's license.

In 1922, she became the first African-American woman to make a public flight.

Bessie returned to the United States. She wanted to open a flying school for African Americans. She hoped to earn the money for it by stunt flying and performing aerial tricks in a rickety plane.

But just four years after making history, on April 30, 1926, she was killed during a rehearsal for an aerial show.

She was 34 years old.

Bessie Coleman taught us to not let anyone keep you from your dreams. That is how a little girl went from toiling in the fields to flying in the sky.

FREDERICK DOUGLASS

· ·

Frederick Douglass would grow up to be one of the most famous abolitionists and orators in history, a man who owned a newspaper and was friends with Harriet Tubman.

But when Frederick Augustus Washington Bailey was nine years old, he was enslaved. And he was taken away from his family several times to work at different plantations.

He eventually wound up on a plantation in Baltimore, Maryland, where he helped care for the plantation owner's children. One of the turning points of his life was when the plantation owner's wife began teaching him to read.

Her husband made her stop because it was

against the law. But that did not stop young Frederick. He borrowed books from white children and picked up flyers and old newspapers from the street. He did not just teach himself to read. He also began teaching other slaves, too.

The more Frederick learned, the worse he felt about being enslaved. After an argument with the plantation owner, he was sent away to be trained to be obedient. The trainer beat Frederick every week. But one day, Frederick, who had grown bigger, had had enough and would not let the man beat him. So, the man sent him to work in the shipyards.

Frederick was only 16 years old. But the move was life-changing. For the first time in his life, he met Black men who were free. After that, he craved freedom so strongly that he decided to escape. In September 1838, he boarded a train to New York. He used the papers of a free Black sailor.

Soon, the woman he loved, a free woman named Anna Murray, came to New York from Baltimore to be with him.

They eventually moved to New Bedford, Massachusetts. He changed his last name to Douglass so the plantation owner could not find him. And he worked in the shipyards to take care of his family.

Frederick soon learned that people wanted to hear him talk about slavery. They had heard horrible stories and wanted to know if they were true. Frederick knew that people had to understand how bad slavery was if they were going to do something about it. Frederick became a walking testament to what African Americans could do and be. He changed the minds of many people who once believed that Black people were not smart enough to be educated.

Frederick decided to tell his story in a book about his life. His autobiography, *Narrative of the Life of Frederick Douglass, An American Slave,* was published in 1845. It became a best seller. The book helped change public opinion about the abilities of African Americans.

Douglass spent years writing and speaking out to improve the lives of African Americans. He began publishing newspapers, including the *North Star.*

He became so famous that he once showed up at the White House without an appointment—and went in.

It was 1863, the year President Abraham Lincoln signed the Emancipation Proclamation to free African Americans from enslavement. Some formerly enslaved Black men joined the Union Army to fight against the Confederate Army in the American Civil War. Frederick went to the White House to complain to President Lincoln about how Confederate troops were torturing and killing captured Black soldiers.

Frederick made his way through a crowd of white people. They were all waiting to see the president. He sent his card in. Minutes later, the president sent for him.

That year, Frederick did much more. He urged President Lincoln to let even more Black soldiers in the Union Army.

Lincoln did, and more than 180,000 Black soldiers joined and helped win the war.

Frederick became one of the nation's most important voices in the fight for the newly free to be treated equally in America. That meant being able to vote, work, and live in peace.

He became a legend.

But the legend began on a plantation in Maryland with a nine-year-old boy who was determined to read.

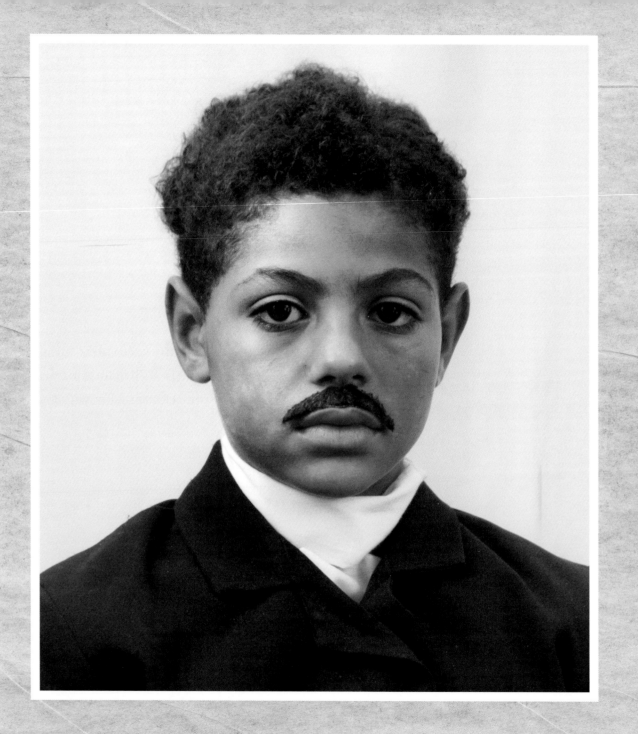

W.E.B. DU BOIS

William Edward Burghardt Du Bois would grow up to be an author, sociologist, historian, editor, professor, internationally known civil rights leader, and the first African American to earn a doctorate from Harvard University in 1895.

But when he was a young boy growing up in a small Massachusetts town, he didn't know how much people would hate him because of the color of his skin.

William was born on February 23, 1868, in Great Barrington, Massachusetts. When his father left, his mother raised him alone on her father's farm outside of town. The family was poor, but his mother provided William with everything he needed to succeed in school.

He attended classes with white students. But he did not know bigotry until one day when a young girl refused a card from him because he was different.

After high school, William sought refuge in education. He attended Fisk University in Nashville. There, he met southern students who talked to him about African Americans enslaved in the South. He learned about the brutal treatment they endured.

William believed that education was the key to a better life for the formerly enslaved. He decided to become a living example. In 1888, he won a scholarship to Harvard University and graduated with top honors. He began to travel in Europe, where he didn't experience the racial prejudice he did in America.

He later married Nina Gomer and began teaching at Wilberforce College in Wilberforce, Ohio. In 1897, he moved to Georgia to teach at Atlanta University. He established the sociology department and taught political science, history, and economics.

William published a collection of essays on being Black in America called *The Souls of Black Folk*. He wrote about the plight of African Americans who must have a foot in two worlds: one Black and one white. He said that Black people had to act a certain way around white people and a different way around Black people. William said that Black people had to have double consciousness and feel like their identity was split into different parts.

"One forever feels his two-ness—an American, a Negro; two souls, two thoughts, two unreconciled strivings; two warring ideals in one dark body, whose dogged strength alone keeps it from being torn asunder," he wrote.

William became famous across the country for being the leader of the Niagara Movement. That was a group of African-American activists who were fighting for equal rights for Black people. The group urged African Americans to aspire to the highest levels of education.

William and his movement were at odds with a philosophy taught by another African-American leader, Booker T. Washington. Booker created the Atlanta Compromise. It was an agreement between African Americans and white leaders that white leaders would provide basic education and jobs to Black people if Black people agreed to segregation and white political rule.

William thought the compromise meant that Black people would become second-class citizens. He wanted Black people to participate fully in politics and be equal to white people. He believed that one of every ten African Americans could become the best and brightest of the race. He called them "the talented tenth" and said they could excel as much as white people. William did not believe in a focus on career education the way Booker did.

In 1909, William helped found the NAACP to fight racial discrimination. The NAACP wanted to make sure that Black people had political, educational, social, and economic equality.

The following year, William stopped teaching to work with the NAACP full time. In a single year—1911—he traveled around the country and spoke to 35,000 people about Black equality.

After decades of fighting discrimination, William decided that the NAACP should work toward Black economic development instead of scholastic achievement. He left the NAACP and spent the rest of his life studying various ways to make sure Black people were employed and able to gain wealth.

W.E.B. Du Bois demonstrated persistence and taught us that building an America without racism is worth the fight.

DUKE ELLINGTON

· ·

Edward Kennedy "Duke" Ellington would grow up to be one of the most celebrated musicians and composers in history. He is considered one of the founding fathers of American jazz.

But when Edward was 15 years old, he was serving sodas at the counter at the Poodle Dog Café and writing his first composition called "Soda Fountain Rag." And he did it before learning to read or write music.

Edward was born on April 29, 1899, in Washington, DC, to pianists James and Daisy Ellington. His mother placed him in piano class by the time he was seven. But he was more interested in baseball, until he snuck into a pool hall when he was 14 and listened to famous piano players like Eubie Blake.

Soon, Edward was imitating ragtime pianists. His high school music teacher gave him private piano lessons. He had found his career.

Meanwhile, he picked up a nickname, thanks to his mother making him use proper manners and etiquette. A friend told him he acted like a nobleman and began calling him "Duke."

The name stuck, and Duke soon began playing in clubs and cafés. At 17, he dropped out of high school three months before graduation to play full time.

When he was 19, he married his childhood sweetheart, Edna Thompson. In 1923, the couple and their son, Mercer, moved to New York. There, he painted signs by day and played with his band, The Washingtonians, at night.

Four years later, he got his big break. A famous band was supposed to play at the legendary Cotton Club in Harlem. The Cotton Club was segregated, but it allowed Black entertainers to play for white audiences. It was one of the most popular clubs in New York.

When the famous band canceled, Duke's band played.

They were so popular that Duke's band soon became a full orchestra—and Duke's orchestra played the Cotton Club until 1931.

The orchestra left New York and went on a world tour. Duke wrote more than 2,000 compositions and gave more than 20,000 performances around the world. Some of his songs are called classics, and they are played and sung today: "Take the A Train," "Satin Doll," "Do Nothing Till You Hear from Me."

When Duke died in 1974, Mercer became the orchestra leader. The music never stopped.

And his father's last words? "Music is how I live, why I live and how I will be remembered."

Duke Ellington taught us that if there is something you love to do, make that your career.

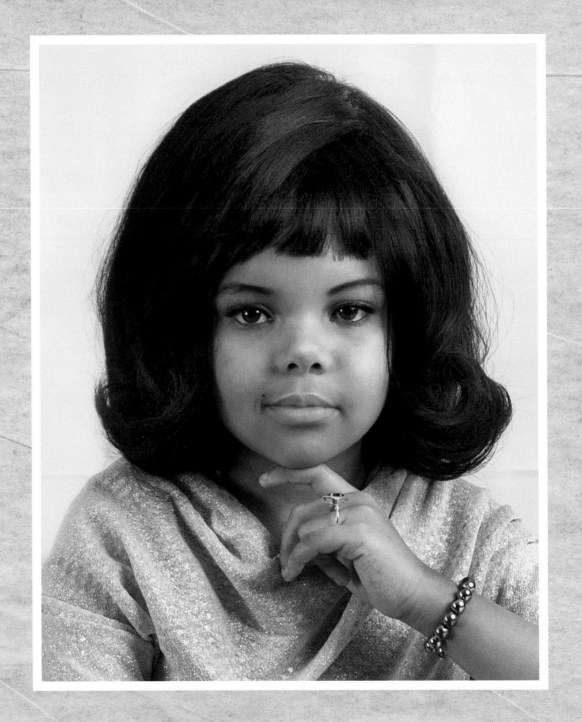

ARETHA FRANKLIN

Aretha Louise Franklin would grow up to become the Queen of Soul, an international R&B singing sensation and a quiet civil rights leader who helped African Americans gain equality.

But when Aretha was 12 years old, she was pregnant.

If there ever was an example of rising above your circumstance, Aretha was living proof of it. She was born on March 25, 1942, in Memphis, Tennessee, to Barbara, a singer and pianist, and the Reverend Clarence L. Franklin, a nationally famous Baptist minister known by his initials, C. L.

When Aretha was two, the family moved to

Buffalo, New York. Three years later, the family moved to Detroit. But the Franklins split up when Aretha was six. Barbara moved from Detroit back to Buffalo, leaving her husband and four children. Aretha was devastated. But she and her siblings visited their mother regularly, or their mother would come to Detroit to see them.

In Detroit, Aretha's grandmother and family friends like Mahalia Jackson helped take care of Aretha and her siblings.

Aretha's mother died of a heart attack on March 7, 1952, just weeks before Aretha's tenth birthday. Her death hit Aretha hard. She found comfort in singing alongside her father, who toured churches around the country. Reverend Franklin was known as the man with the "million-dollar voice."

But two months before her thirteenth birthday, Aretha stopped working to give birth to her first son, Clarence. Still, she didn't stop singing. Her grandmother helped raise him while she went back on the road with her father. Just before her fifteenth birthday, she had her second son, Edward.

She still kept singing. And the little girl who started out great became magnificent. The next year, when she was a sophomore, Aretha dropped out of high school and began singing full time.

Her father had managed her singing career for years. He recorded her songs in the studio at his church.

By the time she was 16, Aretha was touring with the Reverend Dr. Martin Luther King Jr.

When she turned 18, after years of singing gospel, Aretha decided that she wanted to sing popular music. She moved to New York with her father's blessing and signed with Columbia Records. Aretha wasn't defying her father by moving from gospel to R&B. She was following a path he had already carved.

The famous gospel singer James Cleveland once said he "saw Aretha's daddy as one of the few preachers powerful enough to dispel that old myth that says gospel and blues are mortal enemies. He had the courage to say that they actually go together as proud parts of our heritage as a people."

And there was no denying Aretha's talent. In her biography *Respect*, her brother Cecil said: "When you listen to the early things that Aretha recorded, you realize that it's all there—all her musical intelligence. Since we were all raised in the same household by the same dad, it makes sense that we'd all have that same intelligence, but we don't. She was born with it."

The songs that Aretha recorded for Atlantic Records are iconic and timeless. They include "Respect," "Chain of Fools," and "(You Make Me Feel Like) A Natural Woman."

But Aretha was never just a singer. She believed in helping others. She did more than sing during the civil rights movement to fight for equal rights for Black people. She helped fund the movement. She sometimes provided the money to help make payroll. And she gave concerts to raise bail money for activists arrested for protesting racism.

So, Aretha became a vocalist, musician, civil rights activist, global icon, and mother.

She made American history—and she made music history.

She had 112 singles hits on *Billboard* magazine's charts of the most popular songs in America. She had more songs on the Billboard charts than any other female artist.

She won 18 Grammy Awards, including eight in a row for best female R&B vocal performance between 1968 and 1975.

In 1987, she became the first woman to be inducted into the Rock & Roll Hall of Fame.

In 2005, President Barack Obama presented her with the Presidential Medal of Freedom.

In 2010, *Rolling Stone* magazine named her first on the list of "100 Greatest Singers of All Time."

Aretha Franklin taught us to not let our dreams be derailed by circumstances. And no matter what you do for a living, help others.

FANNIE LOU HAMER

· ·

Fannie Lou Hamer would grow up to be a powerful activist in the civil rights movement who fought for the right of Black people to vote.

But when she was 12 years old, she was Fannie Lou Townsend, the youngest of Jim and Lou Ella Townsend's 20 children in a family of sharecroppers.

Her family didn't know it, but Fannie, who was born on October 6, 1917, was meant to be an activist. It would be years before she would start that mission, but when she did, she helped change the country.

When Fannie Lou was a child, she and her family were living in extreme poverty in Ruleville, Mississippi. They picked cotton in the heat, from sunrise to sundown, to

41

give to the man who owned the land where they lived. Her mother did not let the owner beat her children and taught them to be proud that they were African American.

Fannie Lou didn't just work. She attended school, and she loved it. But it was taken away from her when she was 12.

The family had spent years saving enough money to rent land and create a farm. The family moved into their own house. It was just a shack, but it was their own place. They took care of a few animals and just wanted to live in peace.

But some white neighbors who didn't like to see Black people do well, fed poison to Jim Townsend's animals. They had to move. So the entire family returned to sharecropping. That included Fannie Lou, who had to drop out of school to help.

She vowed to help make things better for Black people. She told her mother, "When I get my chance, Mama, I'm gonna do somethin' to right this wrong."

After her mother died, Fannie Lou married Perry Hamer and moved to the plantation in Ruleville where he lived. Fannie Lou and her husband worked hard, adopted two children, and remained in Ruleville.

Fannie Lou might have gone on for many more years just living in Ruleville. But in the early 1960s, the civil rights movement was making its way across the state of Mississippi. It arrived in Ruleville with members of the Southern Christian Leadership Conference and the Student Nonviolent Coordinating Committee.

Fannie Lou listened to the speeches and heard freedom songs for the first time. She realized that she had found a way to keep the promise she had made to her mother: to make things right.

Fannie Lou volunteered to register to vote at the county courthouse. She was one of 18 African-American people who got off the bus at the courthouse. They were met by the police.

When they entered the courthouse, the county clerk staff asked them questions that white residents did not have to answer. Fannie Lou was asked "to copy and interpret a part of the Constitution of Mississippi."

"I hadn't even known Mississippi had a constitution," she said years later.

None of the Black volunteers was allowed to register.

When she got home, Fannie Lou learned that she had been fired from the plantation where she had worked for 18 years. She was forced to leave with her children. Her husband was not allowed to go.

She stayed with friends. On the tenth night at their house, someone fired 16 gunshots into the house. Everywhere she lived, Fannie Lou was harassed. White men carrying rifles rode back and forth in front of every house where she stayed.

She didn't know peace. But she didn't give up.

She took a position with the Student Nonviolent Coordinating Committee. A few months after her first attempt to vote, she tried again.

"You'll see me every 30 days until I pass," she told the county officials.

It took almost three years.

Just six months after she registered to vote, while she was working to register other Black residents, she and other civil rights workers were detained in Winona, Mississippi, and beaten badly. Dr. Martin Luther King Jr. sent Andrew Young, a future mayor of Atlanta and United Nations ambassador, and James Bevel to take her to a doctor in a nearby town. There, the staff washed off Fannie's blood and stitched her wounds. She was left with a severely damaged kidney, a permanent limp, and a blood clot behind one eye.

As soon as she could walk, she began registering voters again. She would later tell *Ebony* magazine that she would not leave the state where her parents and grandparents worked so hard.

"I don't want equal rights no more. I don't want to be equal to men that beat us. I want human rights."

In 1964, the first year that Fannie Lou could vote, she did more than vote. She ran for Congress. When she went to vote, her name was not on the ballot. She wrote it in herself.

And at that year's Democratic National Convention in Atlantic City, New Jersey, Fannie told the crowd about brutality she and others faced for trying to vote. She famously said, "All my life I've been sick and tired. Now I'm sick and tired of being sick and tired."

The next year, Fannie Lou marched beside Dr. Martin Luther King Jr. from Selma to Montgomery, Alabama, to fight for Black people's right to vote.

In 1968, Fannie Lou went to the Democratic National Convention in

Chicago, where Mississippi's all-white delegation was fighting to keep Fannie Lou's delegation from participating. But Fannie Lou prevailed and the Democratic leadership agreed that her delegation, the Mississippi Freedom Democratic Party, had to be seated.

As she took her seat, Fannie Lou Hamer got a standing ovation.

When she got older, Fannie Lou continued to help others. She created the Freedom Farm Cooperative, which fed hundreds of people. It grew into a community with homes available to Black and white residents. Eventually, 5,000 people worked for the cooperative. She also opened a day care center.

As she reached her 50s, Fannie Lou's health began to fail. She was hospitalized in 1972 for exhaustion and in 1974 for a nervous breakdown. In 1976, she was diagnosed with breast cancer.

The next year, Fannie Lou died. Her memorial was so full the town held an overflow service at the high school. There, in front of 1,500 people, Andrew Young said, "None of us would be where we are now had she not been there then."

Fannie Lou was buried in her tiny hometown of Ruleville. But she taught America that freedom belongs to every American no matter where or when they lived.

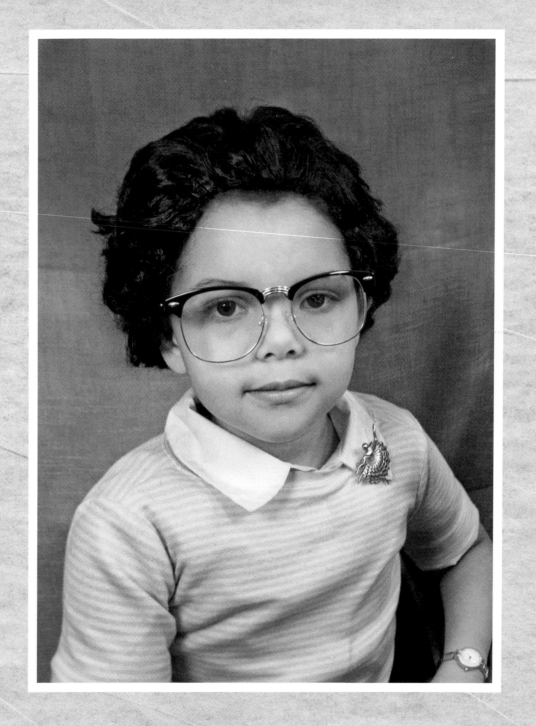

KATHERINE JOHNSON

Creola Katherine Coleman would grow up to be a brilliant mathematician whose work as a "human computer" helped NASA send a man into space.

That is not surprising since, when Katherine was 10 years old, she was smart enough to begin high school when her friends were still in elementary classes.

But there was no school past eighth grade for African-American children in segregated White Sulphur Springs, West Virginia, where she and her family lived. So her parents, Joshua, a farmer, janitor, and handyman, and Joylette, a former teacher, moved the family to Institute, West Virginia. Katherine and her siblings attended classes on the campus of West Virginia State College, now West Virginia State University, in Institute.

Katherine, who was born August 26, 1918, loved math so much that she would count everything when she was a child, she later told reporters when she was an adult.

"I counted the steps. I counted the plates that I washed . . . how many steps from our house to church," she once said.

She said her math skills were a gift from her father. He worked in lumberyards and "could calculate boards that could be cut from a tree and calculate arithmetical problems that confounded some teachers," she said.

Katherine graduated from West Virginia State at 18. She had been thinking about studying English or French. But a professor told her she would make a "great research mathematician."

After college, she became a teacher, one of the professions most available to Black women.

Katherine stopped teaching in 1939 when she married James Goble. But she decided to go back to school and became the first African-American woman to attend graduate school at West Virginia University in Morgantown, considered the state's flagship school.

Then she quit to start a family.

When her children got older, Katherine began looking for work. It happened to be the same time that the U.S. military was looking for people to work in its defense and space programs. Black female mathematicians began answering ads posted on bulletin boards. They thought the work would be more interesting than nursing or teaching.

Katherine applied for a job at the Langley Memorial Aeronautical Laboratory in Hampton, Virginia. She was hired as a research mathematician in 1953 and later became part of the NASA space program.

Katherine's math skills helped her career at Langley. She worked in a pool of women who performed math calculations. She and the other women were called "computers who wore skirts." Their main job was to read the data from airplane black boxes, the devices that record a plane's movements.

One day, Katherine was assigned to help the all-male space flight research team. Her knowledge of analytic geometry was so great, "they forgot to return me to the pool," she later said.

Katherine became known for doing manual calculations herself rather than using a computer. She calculated launch windows, or when a spacecraft could take off. She also calculated the emergency paths for the safe return of Project Mercury rockets. And she performed calculations for the Apollo missions that would eventually take men to the moon.

Despite their brilliance, Katherine and other African-American "computers" were victims of racism. They worked in a different area than white women. They had to use a separate bathroom far from their workstations. And they had to sit at a cafeteria table with a sign that read "Colored Computers."

None of that stopped Katherine.

She said she ignored the way she and others were treated. And she excelled even though she had to force her way to equality. She even had to ask to be included in meetings where her work was being discussed but women were not allowed.

She said she "didn't feel the segregation at NASA, because everybody there was doing research. You had a mission and you worked on it, and it was important to you to do your job . . . and play bridge at lunch. I didn't feel any segregation. I knew it was there, but I didn't feel it."

But she later insisted that she be treated the same as men.

"We needed to be assertive as women in those days—assertive and aggressive—and the degree to which we had to be that way depended on where you were," she said. "I had to be. In the early days of NASA women were not allowed to put their names on the reports—no woman in my division had had her name on a report."

But one day, Katherine's supervisor said her team had to finish a report before they could leave. Her white colleague had to go, so he said, "Katherine should finish the report; she's done most of the work anyway."

Katherine knew she had her chance.

"I finished the report and my name went on it, and that was the first time a woman in our division had her name on something," she later recalled.

Katherine's story—and that of other African-American women who worked with the space program—might have been lost forever. But two things happened: A diligent researcher going through the NASA archives found a 1943 photograph that featured lots of men and a few women at Langley. And Margot Lee Shetterly decided to write a book about the women she'd heard about when she was a child. That book was called *Hidden Figures*. It was made into a movie in 2016.

"Growing up in Hampton, the face of science was brown like mine," said Shetterly, who grew up in the area.

Katherine's greatest moment came when she did the math calculations for astronaut John Glenn's flight right before he became the first American to orbit Earth in 1962. Glenn was given computer data about his ship's orbit path, but he would not take off until Katherine verified the orbit path manually.

"So, the astronaut who became a hero, looked to this black woman in the still-segregated South at the time as one of the key parts of making sure his mission would be a success," Shetterly wrote in *Hidden Figures*.

Katherine continued working with the space program until 1986. President Barack Obama awarded her the Presidential Medal of Freedom.

She lived to talk about the history she made.

Katherine Johnson taught us to not let someone else's bigotry keep you from doing what you were meant to do, from your chance to make history.

BARBARA JORDAN

Barbara Charline Jordan would grow up to be an American lawyer, professor, civil rights leader, and brilliant orator who was the first southern, African-American woman elected to the U.S. House of Representatives.

But when Barbara was a student at Houston's Phillis Wheatley High School, she was planning to be a music teacher until she heard Edith Sampson, a Black female attorney, give a powerful speech. From that moment, Barbara decided to pursue a different dream.

She wanted to be a leader.

Barbara, who was born February 21, 1936, to the Reverend Benjamin Jordan and Arlyne Jordan, a Sunday school teacher, graduated high school in the top 5 percent of her class. She attended the all-Black Texas Southern University because the University of Texas at Austin, where she wanted to go, did not allow Black students.

At Texas Southern, she defeated opponents from Yale and Brown universities to become a national champion in debate. After graduating magna cum laude, she went to Boston University School of Law. Barbara graduated in 1959 and taught for a year before returning home to Houston.

She started her law practice on her father's kitchen table and began her dual career in law and leadership.

She ran for a seat in the Texas Legislature twice and lost both times. But in 1966, she ran for a senate seat and won. She became the first African-American Texas senator since 1883 and the first Black woman ever to serve in the Texas Senate. During her tenure, Barbara sponsored or co-sponsored nearly 70 bills.

Barbara had already made history. But in 1972, she made news. Barbara gave a powerful keynote speech to open the 1976 Democratic National Convention, the first woman to deliver a keynote speech at the gathering. Two years later, she gave a speech to open the impeachment against President Richard Nixon. Congress was trying to determine Nixon's involvement in a break-in at the Democratic National Committee headquarters at the Watergate office complex in Washington, DC. Barbara's speech has been called one of the best of the twentieth century.

As a congresswoman, Barbara sponsored or co-sponsored more than 300 bills or resolutions, including the law that required banks to lend money to poor and minority people.

Unfortunately, Barbara's career stalled when she was diagnosed with multiple sclerosis in 1973. Her illness kept President Bill Clinton from nominating her to the U.S. Supreme Court. She retired from politics in 1979 and began teaching ethics at the University of Texas at Austin. In 1994, President Clinton awarded her the Presidential Medal of Freedom. She received more than 20 honorary degrees from institutions across the country, including Harvard and Princeton.

Words matter, and Barbara's did in so many ways throughout her life.

She died at age 59. But she made history—even then. She was the first African-American woman to be buried in the Texas State Cemetery.

Barbara Jordan taught us that you are never too young to choose to be a leader.

MARTIN LUTHER KING JR.

· ·

Dr. Martin Luther King Jr. would grow up to be one of the greatest civil rights leaders in American history, a man who preached against violence and for equal opportunity for all.

But when he was 12 years old, he tried to kill himself.

It was 1941. Martin was living in a middle-class Atlanta home with his siblings and parents, the Reverend Martin Luther King Sr. and Alberta Williams King. The home was filled with Bible readings and gospel songs. But the family lived in a city where Black children learned early the hard lessons of bigotry.

Six years earlier, Martin's best friend, a white boy, told Martin that he could no longer play with him because he was Black. White and Black children attended separate schools. Adults had to use different entrances into buildings, drink from separate water fountains, and sit in separate sections on city buses.

Young Martin's life changed that year when he snuck away from home without his parents' permission to watch a parade. While he was gone, his beloved grandmother had a heart attack and died. When Martin returned home and learned what had happened, he jumped from a second-story window to try to end his life.

It would be one of the few times he would use violence, even against himself, to solve a problem.

Martin was born on January 15, 1929, the middle child between a sister, Christine, and a brother, A.D. He sang in the church choir and learned from his father to not accept second-class citizenship, protesting when possible, resisting when necessary.

He was on the debate team in high school. He and his teacher traveled to nearby Dublin, Georgia, for an oratory contest sponsored by the Negro Elks Club. He won first prize. On the bus ride home, a white passenger got on. The driver told Martin to get up. He didn't want to, but his teachers made him so he wouldn't get in trouble. It was "the angriest I've ever been in my life," he later said.

Martin also faced a crossroads in his Christian life. He grew up in the church. But as a teenager, he was at odds with his father over the church. He began to doubt the beliefs his family lived by.

But before long, he changed his mind and embraced Christianity.

He was an outstanding student and skipped the ninth and the twelfth grades. As a junior, he was allowed admission to Morehouse College by passing an entrance exam.

The summer before his senior year, he decided to become a minister. He was 18 years old.

Martin was following in the footsteps of his father, grandfather, and great-grandfather. In 1951, he graduated from the seminary where he had been student body president. He briefly considered marrying a white woman until friends convinced him it would keep him from becoming pastor of a Black church.

He later met and married Coretta Scott. She would become his life-long, sometimes silent, partner in fighting for civil and equal rights for Black Americans.

He became pastor of Dexter Avenue Baptist Church in Montgomery, Alabama, in 1954 when he was 25. Just a year later, he helped orchestrate a bus boycott in Montgomery. It was the first major protest of the civil rights movement.

In March 1955, 15-year-old Claudette Colvin refused to give up her bus seat to a white man. It was illegal for Black people to refuse to accommodate whites. Claudette was arrested, but Black leaders decided she wasn't the best test case for challenging the law.

Nine months later on December 1, 1955, 42-year-old Rosa Parks, a seamstress who also worked in the movement, refused to give up her bus seat to a white person. She also was arrested.

The civil rights leaders had their case, and Dr. Martin Luther King Jr. helped lead the Montgomery boycott of the bus system. Black people stayed off the buses for 381 days. Then the NAACP Legal Defense Fund sued and won on behalf of Claudette and others. And racial discrimination on all public buses ended in Montgomery.

Rosa became nationally known. But King became a national leader.

In 1957, Martin joined other civil rights leaders to form the Southern Christian Leadership Conference to organize Black churches. They wanted congregations across the country to join in and participate in nonviolent protests.

Martin began to write books and to talk to large crowds around the country.

With fame came danger.

In September 1958, Martin was signing his book *Stride Toward Freedom* in a department store in Harlem, New York, when a mentally ill woman who thought he was working with Communists stabbed him in the chest with a letter opener. It took him weeks to recover. But he got right back to work.

In 1962, Martin co-wrote a plea to President John F. Kennedy to issue a second Emancipation Proclamation. Kennedy did not. Meanwhile, the Kennedy administration began investigating Martin. The FBI even tapped his phone.

Martin did not let that stop his work. He continued fighting against

Jim Crow laws, a system that kept segregation in place. News organizations began showing how Black people were mistreated. Many white Americans finally began to care about civil rights.

Despite his hard work, Martin faced more criticism. And it wasn't just from white people or the government. Some Black leaders opposed his leadership. Malcolm X and Stokely Carmichael didn't agree with his calls for Black and white people to live together.

But Martin still didn't stop. He went to jail in Birmingham, Alabama, for protesting how Black people were treated. Martin wanted people to get arrested. But white authorities were brutal, attacking protestors with fire hoses and dogs. Still, the protests worked because Americans across the country saw the treatment. Many people were shocked and angry.

In jail, Martin wrote a message to America, his famous *Letter from a Birmingham Jail*. It told protestors to take the movement to the courts.

"We know through painful experience that freedom is never voluntarily given by the oppressor; it must be demanded by the oppressed," he wrote. He cited the Boston Tea Party, which happened during the American Revolution, as evidence that rebellion works.

He also chastised white Americans who were not helping the cause.

A few months later, Martin stood under a hot August sun in Washington, DC, and offered America a new idea. He gave his most famous speech, "I Have a Dream," during the March on Washington for Jobs and Freedom. Some Black leaders still opposed Martin's effort. They said it made it look like white and Black people were working together when they were not really doing so.

But they were.

More and more people joined the movement every month and every year.

Martin finally caught the attention of the world in 1965 after peaceful citizens tried to march from Selma to Montgomery, Alabama. America watched on television as police brutally attacked the peaceful marchers so they could not get to Montgomery to register voters.

The day became known as Bloody Sunday.

Martin was not there for Bloody Sunday. But he organized a second march that also was turned back. Weeks later, a third march was successful. The protestors made it all the way to the courthouse in Montgomery. Martin gave a speech called "How Long, Not Long." He said that the fight would be over soon because "the arc of the moral universe is long, but it bends toward justice."

Over the next three years, Martin traveled all over the country, particularly to northern states. But he also drew more enemies and critics as he began to speak out against the Vietnam War.

In January 1968, Martin began organizing a march on Washington against the war.

He also began organizing the Poor People's Campaign, which would bring people together to fight for the rights of all poor people. Some leaders quit the movement because they felt the needs of Black people were being watered down in such a broad mission.

In March, Martin traveled to Memphis, Tennessee, to support Black sanitation workers. They had been on strike for two weeks because they were underpaid.

On April 2, Martin led a march that was cut short when teenagers began breaking store windows. Those teens later claimed they were paid to disrupt the march.

The next day, Martin gave his final speech, "I've Been to the Mountaintop."

Well, I don't know what will happen now. We've got some difficult days ahead. But it doesn't matter with me now. Because I've been to the mountaintop. And I don't mind. Like anybody, I would like to live a long life—longevity has its place. But I'm not concerned about that now. I just want to do God's will. And He's allowed me to go up to the mountain. And I've looked over, and I've seen the Promised Land. I may not get there with you. But I want you to know tonight, that we, as a people, will get to the Promised Land. And so I'm happy, tonight. I'm not worried about anything; I'm not fearing any man. Mine eyes have seen the glory of the coming of the Lord.

The next day, Martin stood outside his room at the Lorraine Motel, when a shot rang out. Martin fell. He had just told a fellow activist and musician: "Make sure you play 'Take My Hand, Precious Lord' in the meeting tonight. Play it real pretty."

Martin died an hour later after surgery. The stress of his civil rights work became clear after an autopsy. It showed that the 39-year-old leader had the heart of a 60-year-old.

Martin's death sparked riots in cities across America. The city of Memphis ended the strike by giving the sanitation workers more money. President Lyndon Johnson declared April 7 a national day of mourning. The people who attended Martin's funeral heard his voice because his wife, Coretta, asked the church to play his "Drum Major" sermon.

Mahalia Jackson, a celebrated gospel singer and his friend, sang "Take My Hand, Precious Lord."

She sang it real pretty.

Just months after Martin's death, Congress passed the Civil Rights Act of 1968, which banned discrimination in housing. Years later, his widow established the Dr. Martin Luther King, Jr. Center in Atlanta to uphold the ideals that cost her husband his life. Children recite his "I Have a Dream" speech every year.

Martin himself asked people to remember him, not for the Nobel Peace Prize he won but for the work he attempted.

If you want to say that I was a drum major, say that I was a drum major for justice. Say that I was a drum major for peace. I was a drum major for righteousness. And all of the other shallow things will not matter. I won't have any money to leave behind. I won't have the fine and luxurious things of life to leave behind. But I just want to leave a committed life behind.

Dr. Martin Luther King Jr. taught us to be committed to what you believe and be fearless about keeping that commitment.

THURGOOD MARSHALL

Thurgood Marshall would grow up to be an American lawyer who did more than any other person to make life equal for African Americans. He argued more cases before the U.S. Supreme Court than any lawyer in American history. And he became the first African American to sit on the U.S. Supreme Court.

That stellar journey began when Thurgood was 14 years old, and his parents—William Canfield Marshall, a railroad porter, and Norma Arica Williams Marshall, a teacher—made him understand how to use the law to fight for what's right.

His father took Thurgood and his brother to sit and watch the court proceedings so they could learn about cases. Then they would discuss what they had seen. Thurgood later said that his father never told him to become a lawyer, "but he turned me into one. He did it by teaching me to argue, by challenging my logic on every point, by making me prove every statement I made."

Thurgood graduated a year early from Frederick Douglass High School in Baltimore. He attended Lincoln University, an historically Black college in Oxford, Pennsylvania. Among his classmates were Langston Hughes, who would become a celebrated poet, and Cab Calloway, who would become a famous entertainer. Thurgood had planned to study dentistry, but for some reason he put on his application that he planned to study law.

Thurgood was a star debater, but he wasn't a good student. He was suspended twice for playing pranks on other students.

Ironically, in a class at Lincoln, Thurgood voted against the idea of hiring Black professors at his school. But shortly after, he was protesting against an Oxford movie theater making Black and white patrons sit in different sections.

In 1929, he married Vivian Burey and soon became an exceptional student. He graduated with honors with degrees in philosophy and literature. He attended Howard University Law School and studied at the feet of one of the nation's foremost law professors, Charles Hamilton Houston. Thurgood graduated first in his class in 1933 and began forging a path to desegregate a racist America through the courts.

Thurgood's first job was one he created: he opened a law practice in

Baltimore. He began working with the NAACP and focused on school desegregation. In 1936, he joined the NAACP's national staff. For the next few years, he spent most of his time on education cases. He represented a student who was denied admission to a law school because he was Black. Thurgood argued that the school's segregation policy violated the law because Maryland did not provide the same resources at a Black law school.

He won.

When he was 32 years old, Thurgood helped create the NAACP Legal Defense Fund. He began arguing cases to advance civil rights for African Americans. His most famous case was a lawsuit against the school board in Topeka, Kansas. It was on behalf of a young girl who had to walk past a white school every day to attend a Black school that was not as good.

In 1954, Thurgood argued the landmark case before the U.S. Supreme Court, proving that segregated schools violated the U.S. Constitution. He argued that schools separated by color could never be equal. The court agreed and their decision in *Brown v. Board of Education of Topeka* (Kansas) outlawed segregated schools, making it possible for Black and white children to attend the same schools.

In his career, Thurgood argued 32 cases before the Supreme Court. He won 29 of them.

In 1961, President John F. Kennedy appointed Thurgood to the U.S. Court of Appeals for the Second Circuit. Four years later, President Lyndon B. Johnson appointed Thurgood to be the first Black U.S. Solicitor General. That made him the highest-ranking Black government official in U.S. history. Thurgood won 14 out of 19 cases that he argued on behalf of the U.S. government.

On June 13, 1967, President Johnson nominated Thurgood to be the first African-American associate justice of the U.S. Supreme Court. President Johnson said it was "the right thing to do, the right time to do it, the right man and the right place." On August 30, Thurgood was confirmed.

Thurgood, who had spent years using the law to force America to treat African Americans equally, took a seat on the court where he had won so many cases. He described his life's mission this way: "You do what you think is right and let the law catch up."

He sat on the court for 24 years.

But his legacy, even before he took his seat on the high court, was stunning.

He won a case that ended white primaries before general elections (1944).

He won a case that ended racial segregation in interstate public transportation a decade before Rosa Parks refused to give up her seat on a Montgomery, Alabama, bus (1946).

He won a case that ended language in property deeds that kept Black people from being able to buy homes (1948).

He won a case that ended the segregation of America's public schools (1954).

He won a case that ended segregation on buses. That case ended the Montgomery bus boycott (1956).

He won a case that ended the practice of convicting people of a crime for participating in peaceful sit-ins at diners (1961).

Over time, Thurgood would do more to end racist laws than any other person in history.

He won every case while being treated like a second-class citizen himself.

But he did something else. Some of America's most famous attorneys and judges were once his law clerks. That means he helped train a legion of people to continue his mission for justice.

Thurgood retired from the Supreme Court in June 1991. He died four months later and was buried in Arlington National Cemetery.

He left behind numerous papers and notes that represent the collective history of the fight for justice.

But the greater lesson he left for every child is one first articulated by a twentieth-century comedian named W. C. Fields: "It's not what they call you. It's what you answer to." Thurgood provided a solution to America's problems with discrimination. He helped make it possible for Black people to no longer accept second-class citizenship.

And to think, it all began when he was a teenager and his father showed him what a court fight looked like.

Justice Thurgood Marshall taught us that, sometimes, you have to fight. And if you are going to fight, you better be prepared to win—and keep winning.

BARACK OBAMA

Barack Obama would grow up to become the first African-American president of the United States and a popular elder statesman after leaving office.

But when Barack was 15 years old, he was a student at a prestigious college preparatory academy in Honolulu who learned that his family included people from around the world.

Barack was born on August 4, 1961, at the Kapiʻolani Medical Center for Women & Children in Honolulu, just two years after Hawaii became a U.S. state. His mother, Ann Dunham, was a white woman from Wichita, Kansas. His father, Barack Obama Sr., was a Black man from Nyang'oma Kolego, Kenya. His parents met in a class at the University of Hawaii and got married soon after.

After Barack was born, the family moved to Seattle. But the pair divorced, and Barack's father moved back to Kenya. Barack would not see him again for eight years.

"That my father looked nothing like the people around me—that he was black as pitch, my mother white as milk—barely registered in my mind," he wrote in his autobiography, *Dreams from My Father*. He said that his family was "like a little mini-United Nations" because it included American, African, and Asian people.

"I've got relatives who look like Bernie Mac," he said of the popular late, Black comedian. "And I've got relatives who look like Margaret Thatcher" (the white, former prime minister of England).

Barack's mother married again. Her new husband was from Indonesia, a country of more than 17,000 islands in the Pacific Ocean. Eventually, the family moved to Jakarta, Indonesia. Barack attended school and became fluent in Indonesian and had a pet monkey. But despite island life, when asked what he wanted to be when he grew up, he said, "I want to be president."

He was not talking about Indonesia. He was talking about the United States. His mother began to help him focus on his studies. Every morning at 4 a.m., she tutored him in English and taught him about the American civil rights movement.

When Barack was 10, his mother decided that he should move back to Honolulu and live with his grandparents, Stanley and Madelyn Dunham. Barack's experience living in Hawaii and Indonesia affected his view of the world and taught him to respect people from different cultures, he wrote years later.

That same year, Barack's father came to visit. He spoke to his son's class about Kenya, their native country. His father impressed the students, and Barack was proud of him. But after a month, his father was gone.

Barack never saw him again.

Barack entered Occidental College in 1979. Soon, he became active in world affairs. He began to speak out against apartheid, the system of racial segregation in South Africa that kept Black and white people separate. He gave a speech demanding that Occidental not invest in South Africa because of apartheid.

He commanded the audience. He saw the power his words could have.

Two years later, Barack transferred to Columbia University in New York. His course was set. He began studying political science and international relations. He also worked in construction and ran three miles a day.

In 1982, one year before graduation, Barack's father was killed in a car accident. His death made Barack more serious about making a difference in the world.

After he graduated from Columbia, Barack moved to Chicago and worked as a community organizer. He became director of a church-based community group that helped train people for jobs and tutor students to prepare them for college.

In 1988, Barack went to Europe and to Kenya. There, he met some of his father's family for the first time. That fall, he entered Harvard University Law School. He joined the *Harvard Law Review,* and in his second year became the first African-American president of that legal journal.

In 1991, Barack graduated magna cum laude, the second-highest level of achievement, and went back to Chicago. He taught constitutional law at the University of Chicago Law School while writing his first book, *Dreams from My Father.* That same year, he asked Michelle Robinson to marry him. He had met her two years before when he was a summer intern at her law firm, Sidley Austin.

The couple married on October 3, 1992, and eventually had two daughters, who attended the University of Chicago Laboratory Schools.

Barack also increased his activism. He helped the poor, and he oversaw a voter registration campaign to get more African Americans to sign up. His team registered 150,000 voters.

But Barack wanted to do more. So, he ran for the state senate in 1995. He won. In 2000, he reached higher and ran for Congress. He lost. Badly. He went back to the state senate and worked until an opportunity came to run for Congress again.

One of Illinois's senators decided not to run again. And Barack was asked to speak at the August 2004 Democratic National Convention, a meeting of delegates in the Democratic Party from around the country.

He wowed the crowd.

The momentum from that speech helped him win the U.S. Senate race in November. He began working on issues that were important to him like better schools and affordable health care.

But Barack wanted to reach even higher.

He decided to run for president.

Shirley Chisholm tried it in 1972.

The Reverend Jesse Jackson tried it in 1984 and 1988.

Barack defeated Hillary Clinton in the primary or early elections. He accepted the nomination to be president on August 28, 2008, in Denver, Colorado. It was exactly 45 years after Dr. Martin Luther King Jr. gave his "I Have a Dream" speech in Washington, DC.

Barack defeated Senator John McCain to become the first African-American president in U.S. history. He named Hillary Clinton as secretary of state. He attempted to pass policies that matched his motto of "Hope and Change." Among them were efforts to curb global warming and protections for the LGBTQ community. He ordered the execution of the terrorist Osama bin Laden, who was responsible for the 9/11 attacks on the World Trade Center in New York in 2001 that killed thousands of people.

Barack ran for reelection and won again. During his second term, he reestablished a relationship with Cuba, the island nation south of Florida. And he made sure that millions of Americans got health care also known as Obamacare (the Patient Protection and Affordable Health Care Act).

Barack now runs a foundation in Chicago, where his political career started and where he is building his presidential library.

He continues to be presidential, creating entertainment programming for American families and regularly speaking to young people in profound ways, including giving a global commencement speech for students whose 2020 graduations were canceled because of the COVID-19 pandemic.

President Barack Obama taught us that the world is small, and we have more in common than the things that divide us. He also taught us that anything is possible when you have hope and when you want to change the world.

ROSA PARKS AND CLAUDETTE COLVIN

. . . .

Rosa Louise McCauley would grow up to be a civil rights activist who refused to give up her seat on a bus, an action that launched the boycott that ended the segregated bus system in Montgomery, Alabama. She became known as the "Mother of the Freedom Movement."

But when Rosa was 11, she was sent away from her family to live with relatives in Montgomery, Alabama, where she could attend a better school.

Rosa was born in Tuskegee, Alabama, on February 4, 1913, to James, a carpenter, and Leona, a teacher. As a child, Rosa was living in one of the most racist parts of one of the most racist states in America—Alabama. She was constantly reminded of white hatred for Black people.

Her parents separated when she was two years old, and she and her brother went to nearby Pine Level to live on her grandparents' farm.

Rosa loved school and later said that attending Montgomery Industrial School taught her self-respect and dignity.

"We were taught to be ambitious and to believe that we could do what we wanted in life," she said. That self-respect would push Rosa to make history three decades later.

Life under legal racism was hard. Members of a hate group, the Ku Klux Klan, burned crosses in Black people's yards, burned Black churches, and torched the homes of Black people. Her grandfather sometimes slept on the porch in a chair with his shotgun. Rosa slept at his feet.

Her school was set on fire twice. It finally closed, and Rosa went to a different school.

She wanted to be a teacher. But schools in those days focused on teaching girls skills they could use at home: sewing, cooking, and caring for the sick. Schools wanted to make sure that girls could take care of their families or get some kind of job after they graduated.

By the time she was 16, Rosa was helping to run the family home. First her grandmother, then her mother, got sick. Rosa dropped out of school to care for them.

When she was 18, she met Raymond Parks, who was 28. He raised himself because both his parents had died. He was a member of the NAACP, the largest civil rights group in the country. He proposed on their second date, and they got married in 1932. They moved to Montgomery, where Raymond tried to make people care about nine Black teenagers who were falsely accused of attacking two white women in Scottsboro, Alabama.

Rosa earned her high school diploma, a great feat in 1934. She finally got a job at Maxwell Field, an army air base. She rode the bus back and forth from her neighborhood to the base. In 1943, the year her husband left the NAACP, Rosa joined. She became the Montgomery chapter's secretary.

But she did more than take notes. She found lawyers for people who were arrested. She helped people register to vote. Rosa realized that if she was registering other people, she should register as well. She had to take a test and pay a poll tax.

Rosa was upset by how hard life was for Black people. She cleaned houses and did sewing at a department store. And her husband was not well.

Every time she got on the bus to ride to and from work, she was reminded of discrimination. The front was for white passengers; the back was for Black passengers. Black and white passengers could sit in the middle. But if a white person did not have a seat, Black people had to go to the back. And Black and white people could not sit beside each other.

Rosa felt a strong desire to fight for the rights of Black people. She went to a training workshop to learn about racial equality. Rosa was 42 years old. And she was ready to demand change.

Her chance came one cold December day in 1955.

Rosa was working at a downtown department store. When she got off work, she got on the Cleveland Avenue bus to go home. Three stops later, the bus got full and a white man was left standing. The driver ordered Rosa and other Black passengers to give up their seats. The driver told her she'd be arrested if she did not move.

"You may do that," she told him. And she sat still.

The bus stopped, and Rosa was arrested and thrown in jail. She was charged with disorderly conduct.

Within days, word went out that no Black people should ride the bus.

So Black residents—and white supporters—walked.

They walked to work, to school, to church.

They walked everywhere. Some taxi companies charged people what they would have paid to ride the bus—10 cents.

More than 40,000 people participated in the Montgomery bus boycott. They were threatened with beatings and told they would lose their jobs. Some did lose their jobs. But they stayed strong.

For 381 days, near-empty buses rolled around Montgomery.

Rosa was fired.

The following November, the U.S. Supreme Court ruled that segregating city buses was unconstitutional. Rosa's arrest sparked a revolution and made the civil rights movement real for Black and white Americans.

It changed everything, not just about segregation but also for Rosa and Raymond Parks. She received death threats and couldn't get a job. She and her husband moved to Detroit, where her brother lived. Rosa took on speaking engagements and continued her civil rights work until her death on October 24, 2005.

Rosa Parks taught us that self-respect is not a special privilege. Every person, no matter who they are, deserves to be treated fairly.

Claudette Colvin would grow up to be a nurse's aide who lived in the shadow of Rosa Parks.

But on March 2, 1955, when she was just 15 years old—and nine months before Rosa refused to give up her seat on a bus—Claudette got on a bus and was soon told to give up her seat so a white man could sit down. She refused.

She later became one of the plaintiffs in the lawsuit that ended segregated busing.

"It felt like Harriet Tubman was pushing me down on one shoulder and Sojourner Truth was pushing me down on the other shoulder," she told the *Washington Post* years later. "History had me glued to the seat."

Police officers came on board and pulled her from her seat. Claudette fought the charges in court, but she lost. She said Montgomery's Black leaders moved on, looking for a different person or some other way to fight the segregated system.

Claudette got pregnant, felt abandoned, and was nearly lost to history. Civil rights leaders filed a federal lawsuit challenging Montgomery's segregated bus law. They turned to Claudette to join three other women—Susie McDonald, Mary Louise Smith, and Aurelia Browder—as plaintiffs in the case. Claudette agreed.

It was that case that changed the law and ended the Montgomery bus boycott in 1956.

Claudette told news reporters that she heard about the lawsuit's success on the news.

"By then I didn't have much time for celebrating anyway," she told the *Washington Post*. "I had been kicked out of school, and I had a three-month-old baby."

In 1958, Claudette moved to New York and became a nurse's aide. America still might not have known who she was until a newspaper reporter found her and told her story three decades after she took a seat for justice.

Around that same time, she spoke with Rosa Parks for the first time, too. Rosa called and invited her to come and hear her speak.

Claudette didn't go. She couldn't get the day off from work.

Rosa Parks has rightly been called the mother of the civil rights movement.

But the first to refuse to get up was a 15-year-old high school student whose lawsuit changed a system.

Claudette Colvin taught us that you are never too young to make a difference. You are never too young to change the world.

JACKIE ROBINSON

Jackie Roosevelt Robinson would grow up to be the first African American to play Major League baseball in the modern era.

But when Jackie was a 16-year-old high school student, he was a member of a gang.

Jackie was born on January 31, 1919, in Cairo, Georgia, but the family moved to Pasadena, California, when he was a year old. His parents, Mallie McGriff Robinson and Jerry Robinson, were sharecroppers who lived in poverty with Jackie and his three brothers, Edgar, Frank, and Mack, and his sister, Willa Mae.

Mack, a track star who would later win a silver medal at the 1936 Olympics, convinced Jackie to try sports rather than run the streets. So Jackie left the gang and joined almost every team. He ran track, played baseball, tennis, and basketball, and was quarterback of the football team. He was amazing. But while his white teammates and the crowd loved him when he was on the field, they shunned him off the field.

After high school, he attended the University of California, Los Angeles, where he was the first athlete ever to letter in four sports. He won the National Collegiate Athletic Association track and field championship in the long jump. Ironically, his worst sport was baseball.

At UCLA, he met his future wife, Rachel Isum.

Jackie dropped out in 1940, right before graduation, and worked briefly as an assistant athletic director. But sports called, and he began playing football for the Honolulu Bears, an integrated, semipro team. His plan was to play professional football, but the attack on Pearl Harbor on December 7, 1941, derailed those plans. Jackie was drafted in 1942 and sent to a segregated army unit in Fort Riley, Kansas.

There, he was reminded how real racism still was. He and other Black soldiers applied to Officer Candidate School, a training program that would allow them to be promoted. The Black candidates were ignored.

Jackie didn't become an officer until heavyweight boxing champion Joe Louis and others protested. Jackie was commissioned as a second lieutenant.

But on July 6, 1944, racism reared its ugly head in Jackie's life again. He boarded a military bus with whites aboard, and the driver told Jackie to go to the rear. Jackie, like Rosa Parks would 11 years later, said no.

He was arrested and faced a court-martial, a military trial.

Jackie was acquitted of all charges. But the trial kept Jackie from ever going into combat.

After being discharged, Jackie worked on and off the field. He first played football for the Los Angeles Bulldogs. Then he became an athletic director at Samuel Huston College in Austin, Texas.

In early 1945, the Kansas City Monarchs, a Negro Leagues baseball team, offered Jackie a contract for $400 a month. But it didn't last long because Jackie wanted something more stable.

So Jackie tried to do what Moses Fleetwood Walker had done in 1884: play in the Major League. He tried out for the Boston Red Sox in a special event at Fenway Park, but it was a publicity stunt. The team never intended to hire Black players. Boston was eventually the last Major League team to hire Black players.

But another team was serious. Branch Rickey, general manager of the Brooklyn Dodgers, asked Jackie to play for the Dodgers' farm team, the Montreal Royals.

Jackie asked him: "Are you looking for a Negro who is afraid to fight back?" And Rickey told him he wanted a player "with guts enough not to fight back."

Jackie proved that he was the right man for the job.

Jackie faced the anger of white crowds and resentment from Black players in the Negro Leagues who felt they deserved a chance, too. The Negro Leagues had better players, such as Josh Gibson and Satchel Paige.

Jackie also endured the daily racism that most Black Americans faced. He could not stay in the same hotel as his teammates. He had to stay with Black families from town to town. And it was hard to find places to practice. The team once arrived in Jacksonville, Florida, to find the stadium padlocked on game day.

Jackie didn't just endure. He excelled. He was the Minor League's most valuable player. Soon, the crowds began coming to see him.

In 1947, Jackie was called up to the Major Leagues to play for the Dodgers. He played well even though opposing players tried to hurt him, and sometimes did. And his own teammates bullied him.

By the end of the season, he was named Major League Baseball's Rookie of the Year.

Just three years later, in 1950, Jackie's paycheck was the highest of any Dodger ever: $35,000, or $364,474 in 2018 dollars. That same year, Hollywood released a movie about his life, *The Jackie Robinson Story*.

Jackie played himself in the movie.

In 1955, Jackie and the Dodgers beat the New York Yankees to win the World Series.

When Jackie was 37 years old and his career was winding down, he was diagnosed with diabetes. In 1956, the Dodgers traded him to the Giants. But Jackie quit instead and became an executive with a coffee company called Chock Full o'Nuts. He was the first Black vice president of a major corporation. But he still worked in baseball and became the first Black television commentator for Major League Baseball's Game of the Week on ABC-TV.

American baseball was never the same. Jackie had broken the color line. Other Black players joined Major League teams.

Jackie played for only ten seasons. He was Rookie of the Year after his first season and an All-Star for six seasons. He was inducted into the Baseball Hall of Fame in 1962. On June 4, 1972, the Dodgers retired Jackie's uniform number, and in 1997, Major League baseball retired his uniform number 42 on all its teams.

Though he knew he had made history, Jackie said his life was about more than baseball.

He once told another great Black baseball player, Hank Aaron, that "the game of baseball is great, but the greatest thing is what you do after your career is over."

Jackie died of a heart attack at his Connecticut home in 1972, nine days after he threw out the first pitch at that year's World Series.

He was 53 years old.

More than 2,500 people attended his funeral. Thousands of people lined the streets to watch his casket ride to Cypress Hills Cemetery in Brooklyn.

His widow, Rachel Robinson, founded the Jackie Robinson Foundation, which gives scholarships to students and fellows to help them achieve. The foundation plans to open a museum in New York about Jackie and his life, a life much different than it might have been because Jackie decided to trade gangs for sports.

Jackie Robinson taught us that every choice you make affects your future, and it's never too late to change your mind.

HARRIET TUBMAN

Harriet Tubman would grow up to become one of America's greatest abolitionists and political activists and a Civil War spy who escaped slavery and returned to the South numerous times to guide others to freedom.

But when she was a teenager, she was Araminta "Minty" Ross, and she spent her entire childhood enslaved on an eastern Maryland plantation where she was viciously abused.

Once, when she refused to help an overseer tie down a slave to beat him for leaving the plantation without permission, he threw a two-pound iron weight at her and struck her in the head.

It cracked her skull.

For the rest of her life, Araminta suffered abrupt blackouts and hallucinations. That makes what she accomplished for the rest of her life so extraordinary.

Araminta Ross was born into slavery between 1820 and 1822 to Harriet "Rit" Green and Ben Ross. Her mother was held on one plantation while her father was held at another one.

Her mother was a cook, and her father cut timber. Araminta was one of nine children who were torn apart when they were sold to different families. She never saw some of her siblings again.

Araminta would later tell stories about how her mother hid her youngest brother, Moses, from a Georgia trader who tried to buy him. Rit and a network of free and enslaved friends kept him hidden for a month. When the trader and plantation owner finally found him, Rit told him: "You are after my son; but the first man that comes into my house, I will split his head open."

It is believed that Araminta got her spirit of resistance from Rit, whom she would eventually rescue and live with up north.

Growing up, Araminta took care of her siblings. When she was five or six, she began taking care of other children, too.

Once, she was ordered to watch a family's baby sleep. If the baby woke up, she got whipped, which happened five times one morning before breakfast.

She later worked on another plantation. Her job was to check muskrat traps. But she got the measles and had to return to her mother. Later, she went to work in the fields, plowing, hauling logs, and doing other work once done only by men.

She could not read, but Araminta learned words from Bible stories her mother told her. She later told people that the visions she got were not from an injury but were messages from God.

In 1844, Araminta began using her mother's name, Harriet. She married John Tubman, a free Black man. But she was still a slave.

When they had been married five years, Harriet heard that their plantation owner was going to move everyone to a plantation down south, where the treatment of slaves was worse. So that September, she ran. She was 27 years old and took two of her brothers with her. They didn't make it and returned. But Harriet ran away again, on her own. That time, she discovered the Underground Railroad, a network of people who helped runaways.

Harriet made it to Philadelphia before the end of the year. She started a new life. She became a hotel maid. She was free.

But she wasn't happy. She needed her family.

She went back to Maryland to get her family the same year that Congress passed the Fugitive Slave Act. It required people to help plantation owners looking for runaways.

Harriet wasn't afraid of the law. She made at least a dozen trips back and guided at least 70 people to freedom. She became known as Moses, the name of the man in the Bible who led former Jewish slaves out of bondage in Egypt.

She rescued her nieces, three of her four brothers, and her parents. Her husband had married someone else, but she kept everyone else together.

Harriet moved the family to Auburn, New York, where she continued to speak out against slavery. She worked alongside Frederick Douglass, Susan B. Anthony, John Brown, and others fighting against slavery.

But she wasn't done yet. The Civil War between America's northern and southern states began. Harriet volunteered. She first worked as a nurse and cook. She cared for wounded Black soldiers. She also became a spy, helping to report the positions of U.S. Confederate troops.

She was the first woman to lead soldiers on a raid at Combahee Ferry. In her life, she helped rescue hundreds of enslaved people.

When the war ended, slavery was to end. But life was still hard for those formerly enslaved.

Harriet went home to Auburn. But she and her family lived in poverty because the government refused to pay her for her services during the war.

She knew she had to care for her parents and siblings who all lived with her. So she made bricks in her backyard. And she began making speeches on behalf of women's rights.

In 1866, Harriet married Nelson Davis, and they adopted a little girl.

Harriet finally had freedom and her own family.

She continued her activism, fighting for the right to vote for women. She established a home for elderly African-American patients. Near the end of her life, she lived there.

She died in 1913, a half century after the Emancipation Proclamation was issued and seven years before America recognized a white woman's right to vote.

Harriet Tubman, the heroine nicknamed Moses, taught us to not let anyone steal our destiny.

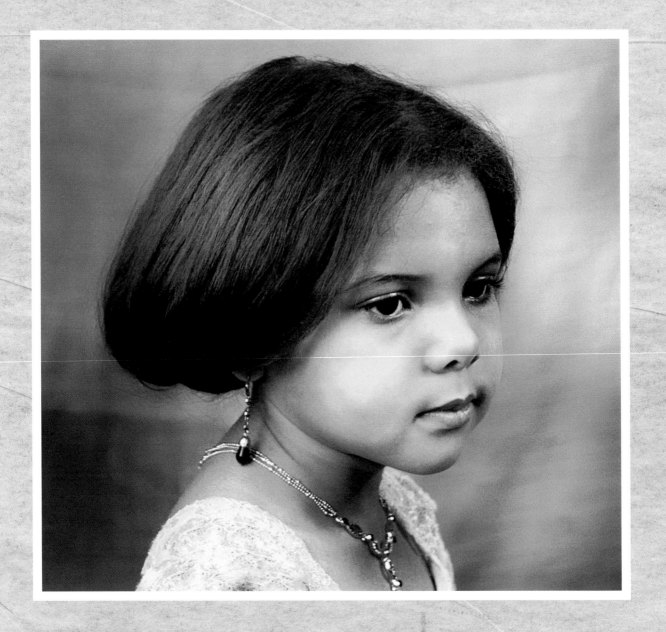

MADAM C. J. WALKER

Madam C. J. Walker was an entrepreneur, philanthropist, and social activist and was one of the first American women to become a self-made millionaire.

But when she was 14, she was Sarah Breedlove—and she was a bride.

Sarah was born on December 23, 1867, the first of Owen and Minerva Breedlove's children to be born free. When she was seven, her parents, sharecroppers near Delta, Louisiana, died of yellow fever, so Sarah moved in with a sister in Vicksburg, Mississippi. She worked as a maid.

"I had little or no opportunity when I

started out in life, having been left an orphan and being without mother or father," she later said.

Sarah married at 14 to escape brutal treatment from her sister's husband. She had a daughter when she was 18. Two years later, her husband, Moses McWilliams, died. She and her daughter moved to St. Louis, where her brothers were barbers. She did laundry for 18 years.

As an adult, Sarah developed a scalp disorder that made her hair fall out. She experimented with hair care treatments to help. In 1905, Annie Turnbo Malone, an entrepreneur selling hair care products for Black people, hired Sarah and moved her to Denver. Sarah soon developed her own hair care treatment and began selling it. Her second husband, Charles Walker, a journalist, advertised her treatment. He encouraged her to call herself Madam C. J. Walker for business reasons. The couple traveled around the South selling the product and showing women how to straighten their hair with pomade and hot combs.

In 1908, the Walkers moved to Pittsburgh, Pennsylvania. Sarah opened a factory and a beauty school. Two years later, she moved what had become the Madam C. J. Walker Manufacturing Company to Indianapolis. There—55 years before Mary Kay Ash founded Mary Kay and began training sellers—Sarah trained beauty consultants to sell her products. These women, called Walker Agents, sold in neighborhoods. They promoted Sarah's motto of "cleanliness and loveliness."

In 1913, after divorcing her husband, Sarah traveled across Latin America and around the Caribbean. She spent that time teaching people the "Walker System" of hair care. When she returned to America three years later, she moved to the Harlem neighborhood of New York.

In 1918, Sarah built Villa Lewaro, a mansion at Irvington-on-Hudson, about 20 miles north of New York.

Sarah made a fortune with her company, and she made sure to give back. She awarded scholarships to students, made donations to the NAACP, and gave funding to other organizations that helped people. She also became involved in the Harlem Renaissance, the artistic movement that was considered a rebirth of African-American arts. The Harlem Renaissance lasted through the mid-1930s and influenced artists and writers across the country. Sarah hosted Renaissance events at Villa Lewaro. Her mansion became a National Historic Landmark in 1976.

Sarah died of hypertension on May 25, 1919, at Villa Lewaro. She was worth between $600,000 and $700,000, the equivalent of more than $9 million in 2019 dollars.

Madam C. J. Walker taught us that if you decide who you want to be, you will live how you want to live.

BOOKER T. WASHINGTON

Booker Taliaferro Washington would grow up to be a professor, educator, author, orator, and adviser to U.S. presidents.

But when he was young, he was a boy without a last name or a birthdate, working enslaved on a plantation in Franklin County, Virginia, whose greatest dream was to learn to read.

Booker was born around 1856 to Jane, an enslaved African-American woman, in a 14-by-16-foot log cabin. He never knew his father, not even his name, but he heard he was a white man from a nearby plantation. His mother was the plantation cook, and their cabin was the plantation kitchen.

In his autobiography *Up from Slavery*, the man

who would become a scholar wrote, "there was no period of my life that was devoted to play."

He was never allowed to go to school. But he remembered carrying the books of a slave owner's daughter to the door of the schoolhouse.

"I had the feeling that to get into a schoolhouse and study in this way would be about the same as getting into paradise," he wrote.

He said he could not remember the family ever sitting together to eat a meal. He did remember that his first shoes were made of wood with rough leather tops.

When the boy who would come to be known as Booker was nine years old, President Abraham Lincoln signed the Emancipation Proclamation ending slavery.

It was no longer illegal for him to learn to read. So, he taught himself.

And he kept learning and teaching his entire life. He became one of the century's greatest fighters for civil rights for the formerly enslaved and continually oppressed. And he turned a former plantation into one of the greatest Black colleges in America.

Booker was convinced that the formerly enslaved could build lives as workers and work alongside white people. He talked about how many of the formerly enslaved did not have hard feelings against plantation owners. He said there were "many instances of Negroes tenderly caring for their former masters and mistresses who for some reason had become poor and dependent since the war."

Booker's belief that Black and white people could get along would last a lifetime.

Booker believed in work, but he also desperately wanted to go to school. He was working in a salt mine when he learned that a new school was going to open. His mother had married, and his stepfather would not let him go because he was needed for work.

By the time Booker could attend classes, he discovered that school would start 30 minutes before he was allowed to leave work. So he set the boss's clock back by 30 minutes so he could be on time. When he could no longer attend during the day, he went to night school.

One day, he learned about a school called Hampton Normal and Agricultural Institute. He vowed to go. And he did. He worked as a janitor to help pay his way.

Booker graduated with honors. He became a teacher in the night school at Hampton. Soon, he was asked to help create a school for Black students in Tuskegee, Alabama. The state legislature provided $2,000 to pay teachers. But it did not provide money for any buildings.

So, Booker and his students started building the Tuskegee campus in a shack and an old church.

The students "were the architects and carpenters of classrooms, dormitories, a church and a curriculum that included everything from farming to printing," according to *100 African-Americans Who Shaped American History*.

That campus became the Tuskegee Normal and Industrial Institute, a college with a $2 million endowment to keep it running. Booker was its leader for 30 years. It is now the historically Black Tuskegee University with an endowment topping $126 million.

Booker also became a leader in the fight for civil rights for the formerly enslaved.

It was hard for African Americans to succeed because southern states created Jim Crow laws to keep Black and white people separated and allowed legal discrimination against Black people. The name came from a caricature of a formerly enslaved man who was the subject of an offensive song called "Jump Jim Crow."

Booker became famous across the nation in 1895 when he proposed something controversial for African Americans. He said that the formerly enslaved could make more progress by getting job training rather than college degrees.

He said this in a famous speech called the "Atlanta Compromise" before a mostly white audience in Atlanta. The compromise was that African Americans would not ask for the right to vote and would not retaliate against racist behavior. It also said that African Americans would tolerate segregation in exchange for free vocational or industrial education.

"The opportunity to earn a dollar in a factory just now is worth infinitely more than the opportunity to spend a dollar in an opera-house," Booker said.

At first, Booker had wide support. But then W.E.B. Du Bois and other Black leaders began to disagree with him. They believed the policy would make Black people second-class citizens. They wanted Black people to have the same rights and political power as white Americans.

But Booker had the support of white leaders, including U.S. presidents. Many historians say his way of dealing with racism helped the civil rights movement. He still believed that African Americans should go to college. But he wanted his fellow citizens who had been enslaved to consider working as a possible alternative.

Booker publicly spoke about Black and white people working together. But he gave money secretly to help lawsuits that fought segregation.

And he sometimes worked alongside Du Bois. They organized a photo exhibit in Paris to show Black students at work, demonstrating that they were contributing to American society.

Booker wrote at least five books, including two autobiographies. The second one, *Up from Slavery*, moved President Roosevelt to invite Booker to the White House. It was the first time a president invited an African American to the presidential residence.

By 1915, Booker wasn't well. His years of building schools and building relationships took its toll. He got very sick while visiting New York City. When doctors told him he was dying, he got on a train and went home to Tuskegee.

Booker died of congestive heart failure on November 14, 1915—a few hours after he arrived. He was 59 years old.

The little boy who chased education created a system that would teach thousands of other African Americans. Booker taught us that education truly is the key to success.

IDA B. WELLS

· ·

Ida B. Wells would grow up to be an investigative journalist, civil rights leader, educator, and activist. Her efforts to end lynching, the crime of hanging Black people from trees, would make her one of the most famous Black women in America.

But when Ida was 16, she lost her parents and a brother to a yellow fever epidemic, and she became head of a household of children.

Ida was one of eight children born to James Wells, a Shaw College trustee and carpenter, and Elizabeth "Lizzie" Wells, a famous cook. Ida was visiting her grandmother Peggy Wells's farm and escaped the plague. Ida did not want her five brothers and sisters split up and sent to live in different places. So she lied about her age and became a teacher and raised her siblings herself with her grandmother's help.

In 1883, Ida's grandmother died from a stroke, so Ida took her two sisters to live with an aunt in Memphis. Memphis was a long way from Holly Springs, Mississippi, where Ida had been born into slavery on July 16, 1862. She was free a year later when President Abraham Lincoln signed the Emancipation Proclamation.

Although Ida became a teacher, she took classes at Fisk University during summer breaks. She knew she was meant for more than teaching and mothering.

In her heart, she was an activist. Soon she would begin speaking out about the mistreatment of Black people, including her own cases. On May 4, 1884, a Chesapeake & Ohio Railroad train conductor told Ida to give her first-class seat to a white passenger and move to the crowded smoking car. The demand was legal. The Supreme Court ruled against the Civil Rights Act of 1875 that would have banned racial discrimination in public accommodations.

But Ida refused to relinquish her seat, just like Rosa Parks would decades later on a bus in Montgomery, Alabama. The conductor and two men dragged her out of the car. Ida wrote about what happened in the *Living Way*, a Black church weekly newspaper. She also sued the railroad. Seven months later, the court granted her $500. But the Tennessee Supreme Court reversed the ruling, saying "her persistence was not in good faith to obtain a comfortable seat for the short ride."

Ida later wrote about her disappointment: "I had hoped such great things from my suit for my people. . . . O God, is there no . . . justice in this land for us?"

As racial violence against Blacks grew worse, Ida's activism grew, and she began to investigate lynchings. Black-owned newspapers across the country carried her reports about this heinous behavior.

For as long as she could, Ida continued her two jobs, teaching elementary school and becoming one of the nation's foremost journalists. But after she became editor and co-owner of the *Free Speech and Headlight*, a Black-owned newspaper, she wrote articles criticizing the conditions of schools attended by Black children. In 1891, the Memphis Board of Education fired her.

Now a full-time journalist, Ida would write regularly about the horrors of being Black in America, something that hit close to home in 1892. Her friend Thomas Moss had opened a grocery store in 1889 in the South Memphis neighborhood called the Curve.

Ida was one of Thomas's closest friends and godmother to his first child.

In March 1892, a young Black boy was playing a game of marbles with a young white boy in front of Thomas's store. They got into a fight and the white boy's father, William Barrett, raced across the street and beat the Black boy. Two of Thomas's employees tried to defend the boy. A simple fight between two boys turned into a battle between adults. The actual reason for Barrett's anger was that Thomas's store, which he co-owned with his friends Will Stewart and Calvin McDowell, had become more popular. The fight escalated and shots were fired back and forth, injuring several white men. Authorities arrested the three Black grocers and stood by when, three days later, a white mob dragged them from the jail, took them to a nearby rail yard and shot them.

Before he died, Thomas said: "Tell my people to go west. There is no justice for them here."

After Thomas's death, Ida told Black people to leave Memphis.

"There is, therefore, only one thing left to do; save our money and leave a town which will neither protect our lives and property, nor give us a fair trial in the courts, but takes us out and murders us in cold blood when accused by white persons."

She began publishing her findings in *Southern Horrors: Lynch Law in All Its Phases*. Ida found that the lynchings happened not because of allegations that Black men had wronged anyone or assaulted white women. They were done to frighten the formerly enslaved and stop Black residents from competing in business with white Southerners.

Ida suggested that Black people arm themselves to defend against lynching. Her second published pamphlet, *The Red Record*, described all the lynchings she could find that had occurred since 1863 when the Emancipation Proclamation freed Blacks from enslavement.

She wrote that most Americans had no idea how much violence was being used against Black Southerners. She wrote that "ten thousand Negroes have been killed in cold blood, [through lynching] without the formality of judicial trial and legal execution."

Her report included 14 pages of statistics along with graphic descriptions of lynchings. But she was smart enough to use the reports of white newspapers for her research so it could not be dismissed.

Black-owned newspapers across the country carried Ida's reports. But Ida didn't feel America was acting quickly enough to stop the scourge. So, she took her anti-lynching campaign abroad. People in Britain were horrified. While she was there, she was asked to write about her campaign and the foreign reactions for the Chicago-based *Daily Inter-Ocean* newspaper. It was the only major, white-owned paper to denounce lynching. The editor, William Nixon, asked Ida to write for the paper from England. That made her the first African-American woman to be a paid correspondent for a mainstream white newspaper.

Ida spent months talking to thousands of people, showing actual photographs of lynchings. Britain was sympathetic to her cause. But newspaper editors across America were not.

The *New York Times* called her "a slanderous and nasty-minded mulatress." It was not enough to hurt her cause or her international recognition.

The more Ida wrote, the more threats she received. A white mob destroyed her newspaper office and presses. She left Memphis and moved to Chicago, where, in 1895, she married Ferdinand Barnett, an attorney and civil rights activist. The *New York Times* reported their marriage on the front page.

The couple had met two years earlier while working on a pamphlet criticizing the lack of Black representation at the World's Columbian

Exposition in Chicago in 1893. That year, Ida began writing for Barnett's newspaper, the *Chicago Conservator*, Chicago's first Black newspaper.

After their marriage, Ida became editor of the paper. They were equals, a state that was unusual at the time. Other activists became resentful, and some women found her behavior unladylike.

Ida was doing her best work at a time when Booker T. Washington and W.E.B. Du Bois were becoming rising stars. Activists were perceived as competing for attention. Ida increased her focus on women's issues and helped women win elective office. In 1896, she, along with Harriet Tubman and others, founded the National Association of Colored Women's Clubs. But even in that, she faced disdain. One organizer, Mary Terrell, said members from Chicago would not participate in a national meeting if Ida was there. The president excluded Ida from the group she helped found.

Ida continued working for women's rights and civil rights until her death from kidney failure on March 25, 1931. The *New York Times* wrote her obituary—in 2018.

Ida B. Wells Barnett taught us that knowing what is right and doing something about it are two different things. Do both.

STEVIE WONDER

Stevland Hardaway Judkins would grow up to become one of the most prolific, commercially successful songwriters, musicians, and entertainers in American history, winning 25 Grammy Awards, and selling more than 100 million albums.

But when he was 11 years old, he was a young, blind singer whose mother knew he was special.

Stevie was born May 13, 1950, in Saginaw, Michigan, to Lula Mae Hardaway, a songwriter, and Calvin Judkins. Stevland was born six weeks early and suffered from a condition that stopped the growth of his eyes.

His parents divorced when he was four and his mother moved her six children to Detroit. She changed Stevie's last name to Morris and nurtured his musical talent. He played harmonica, piano, and drums and sang in the church choir. He and a friend formed a duo that sang at dances and on street corners.

In 1961, a member of a famous singing group called the Miracles heard him sing. The Miracles were among many groups working for Berry Gordy, who founded Tamla Records and Motown Records.

Stevland auditioned for Gordy, who signed him to a contract. A producer changed his name to Little Stevie Wonder.

Stevie's mother received a salary while Stevie got $2.50 a week and a private tutor.

Stevie recorded several songs. But none were big hits.

But when he was 12, Stevie traveled with popular groups on a tour called the Motortown Revue. They played theaters that allowed Black artists to perform. Stevie sang his first hit song, "Fingertips," at a Chicago theater. It became a No. 1 hit on the *Billboard* magazine Hot 100 chart, making Stevie, 13, the youngest artist ever to top the chart.

Most of the songs Stevie recorded next didn't do well, and Gordy was ready to drop him from the Motown label.

So, Stevie grew up. The producers dropped "Little," and he became Stevie Wonder.

He recorded "Uptight (Everything's Alright)," which kept his job. Then he began to write songs for himself and for other groups. He wrote a famous song called "The Tears of a Clown." Smokey Robinson and the Miracles recorded it, and it became a No. 1 hit.

In September 1970, Stevie married a songwriter named Syreeta Wright—the first of three marriages. He and Syreeta attempted to write songs together. But none were hits.

For a while, he worked on his music alone. But in March 1972, he re-signed with Motown. His next album, *Music of My Mind*, did not impress critics. Stevie kept at it, though. He began having hits, and in 1976 he released *Songs in the Key of Life*, which is considered one of the best albums ever recorded. It was the first album by an American artist to make its debut at No. 1 on the Billboard charts. Many of the songs from the album have become standards, sung by many artists many times.

But Stevie wanted to do more than make music. He wanted to help change the world. His most famous campaign was one in 1980 to help make Dr. Martin Luther King Jr.'s birthday a holiday in the United States.

He and supporters around the world succeeded. And the birthday song he wrote for the occasion is now sung for everyday birthdays.

Stevie continued to have great fame in the 1980s. He was on television. He participated in collaborations such as the "We Are the World" recording of stars to raise money for the poor. He recorded a duet with Paul McCartney, formerly of the Beatles. He also wrote songs that appeared in films, including "I Just Called to Say I Love You," which won the Academy Award for Best Song in 1985.

Stevie accepted the award in the name of Nelson Mandela, the Black South African activist who spent 27 years in prison for fighting against apartheid. The South African government then banned Stevie's music from its radio stations in retaliation.

Stevie continues to make music and perform. He sang at President Barack Obama's first inauguration and Michael Jackson's funeral, both in 2009.

And he continues his activism. On April 4, 2018, he joined Twitter. His first tweet was a five-minute video honoring Dr. Martin Luther King Jr.

Stevie Wonder taught us the most important lesson of all: Do not let anyone underestimate what you can do.

Our Thanks

We want to express the sincerest of thanks to:

...everyone who supported us during this journey

...the team at Wayne State University Press—Annie, Emily, Jamie—who work in the heart of Detroit to make authors look good, and the editing team led by Lisa Stallings that makes us all look good

...Lowney and Mr. Bennie Pitt, Rochelle's late, beloved grandparents. She still writes everything to honor them

...Tamara Winfrey Harris, whose advice and wisdom as Rochelle's accountability coach make her life better

...Benet Wilson, who kept the wolves at bay and took over some tasks so Rochelle could finish this one

...and Lola and Caleb, who were infinitely patient while being treated like history dolls in costume and makeup between play sessions, meals, and Fortnite.

About the Authors

Rochelle Riley spent nearly a quarter century as a newspaper columnist before turning her attention to books and public service. An inductee in both the Michigan Journalism Hall of Fame and the North Carolina Media and Journalism Hall of Fame, she won dozens of national and local awards during her journalism career. She is now the director of arts and culture for the City of Detroit and a cofounder of Letters to Black Girls, an initiative to give letters of advice and encouragement from Black women to Black girls across the country. She is the author of 2018's *The Burden: African Americans and the Enduring Impact of Slavery*, about which Kareem Abdul-Jabbar said: "*The Burden* is one of the most comprehensive, enlightening, and thought-provoking books I have ever read on African-American history. The insights into how slavery affects every aspect of America today from politics to economics to culture is powerfully presented by this remarkable essay collection."

Cristi Smith-Jones is a stay-at-home mom turned amateur photographer who lives with her husband and daughters, Lola and Eden (and their cat, dog, and chickens), in Kent, Washington. She enjoys finding creative ways to bring art and history to life for her girls and dedicates her efforts at documenting history to her grandmother, Mary Smith, who died in 2019. "She was the first African-American woman to change MY world," Cristi says.